The Beckoning Isle is the story of the degeneration of a society and the vicious politics of retribution. But it is also a tale of two men, on opposite sides of the battle, united only by the fatalism of their ideologies. Abhay Sapru offers a unique perspective of the Sri Lankan War in an engaging, page-turning account of the clash between the Indian Peace Keeping Force and the LTTE, with voices from both sides of what will go down as one of history's great tragedies.

—*Shashi Tharoor*

The Beckoning Isle is a masterpiece in realistic settings of Sri Lanka during the days of the IPKF. Though it follows the travails of an Indian Special Forces Assault troop crisscrossing the path of an LTTE colonel, it takes you through a bit of history and the whole gambit of politics, intrigue, conflict, human behaviour and the tribulations that surrounded the war between the IPKF and the LTTE. The style of the author who himself was part of the IPKF is excellent and the lucid narration will keep you engrossed to the last word.

—*Lt Gen (Retd) Prakash Katoch*

Abhay Sapru's second book on war from a combat soldier's perspective is the real McCoy. It catches you by the scruff of your neck and doesn't let go till the end. A chapter of the Indian Army's ill-fated adventure into Sri Lanka, fought in dense jungles, against a cornered comrade turned enemy, you can smell the fetid smell of the jungle, mixed with the smell of death, fear, courage and strangely, respect for an enemy who was fighting for its very survival. Only a combat soldier could have written this!

—*Prahlad Kakkar*

THE BECKONING ISLE

Abhay Narayan Sapru
Bestselling Author of *In The Valley of Shadows*

THE
BECKONING
ISLE
THE REAL SPECIAL FORCES STORY

© Abhay Narayan Sapru

First published 2017

All rights reserved. No part of this book may be reproduced, stored in a retrieval system or transmitted in any form or by any means—electronic, mechanical, photocopying, recording or otherwise—without the prior permission of the author and the publisher.

This is a work of fiction and creative liberty has been taken to describe people, events and places.

The map used in this book has been worked upon by the author, is not to scale and is for illustrative purposes only. No copyright infringement is intended.

ISBN 978-81-8328-491-2

Published by
Wisdom Tree
4779/23, Ansari Road
Darya Ganj, New Delhi-110002
Ph.: 011-23247966/67/68
wisdomtreebooks@gmail.com

Printed in India

*To the brave officers and men
of the IPKF who fought in Sri Lanka—
especially those who never made it back.*

*Col and Dolly—your memory never fades.
Ritu, Shradz and Ary—some things never die.
And to brothers in arms—serving and ex—
Pity, the best tales can never be told.*

It is not the critic who counts; not the man who points out how the strong man stumbles, or where the doer of deeds could have done them better. The credit belongs to the man who is actually in the arena, whose face is marred by dust and sweat and blood; who strives valiantly; who errs, who comes short again and again, because there is no effort without error and shortcoming; but who does actually strive to do the deeds; who knows great enthusiasms, the great devotions; who spends himself in a worthy cause; who at the best knows in the end the triumph of high achievement, and who at the worst, if he fails, at least fails while daring greatly, so that his place shall never be with those cold and timid souls who neither know victory nor defeat.

—Theodore Roosevelt

Preface

On a recent trip to Sri Lanka, I remembered the landmark, a milestone next to a big tree from where the path cut into the jungle on the Mankulam-Mannar Road. The place hadn't changed much, except for the shops and the houses, all constructed in the last couple of years and the broad shiny new highway with signboards. The jungle on either side of the road looked as formidable and uninviting as it had years ago and I marvelled at our ability to have penetrated that veritable mass of dense vegetation, mostly at night, to spend days within. The Sri Lankan army never ventured into the jungles, or perhaps they didn't need to, as the LTTE by then had made the cardinal mistake of shedding guerrilla warfare, in which they were masters, in favour of holding ground like a conventional army. An arrogant mistake that led to their final annihilation.

I had told the cab driver to go slow and noticed it immediately. The tree and the milestone looked a bit worn out or so I imagined coming back after well over two decades. But of the path I could see no sign. I got out and walked up and down looking for some indication. The driver eyed me suspiciously and was clearly worried…'Mines Sir,' he warned in a timid whisper. Barely a kilometre back we had passed a demining crew busy marking out the area. A Japanese-aided NGO (DASH) was working in the Mankulam belt. I parted the undergrowth at random and right opposite the milestone ran into luck. An unused path disappeared into the thick jungle. I hesitated just for a second, giving no time for my imaginative mind to conjure up doomsday scenarios, before stepping out onto the path. The driver followed, wondering, as I walked ahead confidently and within twenty minutes hit the cluster of trees where we had halted and taken harbour. I was surprised how quickly we reached, for years back walking the same distance at night had taken nearly three hours.

I cut through the undergrowth and hit the forest fire lane which had been the killing area. Nothing had changed and I stood and studied the ambush site. I could find so many faults with the siting now. It was a catharsis of sorts. My mind latched on to concrete images of the past, as the bush came alive to a group of young men, their faces strained and tired, some dozing, some cleaning their weapons, while the others silently played cards. So much time was spent in the bush that we had learnt to make ourselves comfortable and other than a post, the only other place and time one felt safe was while waiting for the enemy, tucked in a thicket. Memory is like water, once ruffled, the past is stripped and lingers with each ripple. I identified the various spots and recalled incidents and thought I had the right tree under which I stripped.

I was heading for a quick peep through the undergrowth, when agitated red ants started dropping from above, through the gap in between my neck and my shirt's collar and right in. I must have done the fastest Full Monty and had I been Bear Grylls (of *Man vs Wild* fame), I would have eaten the lot, so furious was I with the ants. For the rest of the stay, I recall dreaming up plans to destroy them and even contemplated blowing up the tree. It was nostalgia with a vengeance and I had mixed feelings, as I struggled to justify all the effort, privations and risks we took. Was it worth it? Did I learn anything? Was I a better man for the experience? Did all the time we spend, sitting in the bush in Sri Lanka to Kashmir, contribute in any way to the overall perspective of things, then and now? I was reminded of lines by Emerson:

> *I laugh at the love and the pride of man,*
> *At the Sophist schools and the learned clan;*
> *For what are they all, in their high conceit,*
> *When man in the bush with God may meet?*

Literally taken, only those who kicked the bucket in such operations ended up meeting God. The rest of us went back carrying combat or bush scars, the latter a skin problem caused by a tiny fly in the Sri Lankan jungles, which would get under the skin, often hatching eggs there, making it difficult to pull out. Like a long run, the bush was a place to remember, a place which gave man the freedom of spending time with the mind.

When I was planning my trip, I had read the following on the Sri Lanka tourism website:

'Plan your dream holiday and travel through an island of small miracles. Get a tan, surf, pamper yourself, explore wildlife or find your space.'

'Well,' I thought, 'how time flies! Back then, it was a nightmare trip and the only miracle was, that unlike a lot of others, I came back in one piece. I did get a tan, not that I needed one, and surfing hadn't been invented in the subcontinent I guess. Wildlife explored us on numerous occasions, rather than the other way round and of course, quite a few of us found permanent space on the island. Either way, for those who did a tour of duty in Sri Lanka, the experience would echo through their lives and most, in an inexplicable way, were changed.'

While a plot has been interwoven, most of the incidents, places and experiences are factual. The Jaffna University heliborne operation was conducted in the early part of the conflict, with the aim to neutralise the LTTE leadership. The operation was a debacle with great loss of life on our side. One of the largest clashes with the LTTE took place in March 1989, in the Nayaru Lagoon area, very close to where the end game of the Tamil Tigers was finally played out with the Sri Lankan military in 2010. The skirmishing thereafter, continued for a month, as the Indian Peace Keeping Force (IPKF) threw in a couple of brigades to evict the Tigers from their last strong bastion in the Alampil jungles. Various estimates have been given of the casualties suffered on both sides, ranging from over forty-five killed and wounded on our side, with the Tigers suffering almost the same number, if not more. While the bulk of this fight took place in and around their main camp, as a diversion to ease the pressure in the jungles, the LTTE attacked an Indian Army post at the village of Kumulamunai. The incident has been described in the narrative.

It was with a bit of difficulty that I finally traced out where the camp had been located so many years ago. It was a revelation to discover that the village and hill were much bigger than

I had imagined and in the intervening years, cottages and schools had sprung up all over, as an initiative by some Indian housing organisation. In fact it was an old local watching me curiously walk up and down the path in desperation, who pointed at a bush covered hillock with a new temple on top. 'IPKF post Sir,' he said. 'We built the temple after the Indians vacated,' he conveyed through the interpreter, a soldier who had accompanied me from the nearest Sri Lankan army post at Alampil.

The Indian Army went into Sri Lanka as a peacekeeping force and in no time got embroiled in an intense protracted guerrilla war. The IPKF managed to establish its will by sheer bulk and the so-called peace was never tenacious and was maintained at a very heavy price in life and material. Untrained in fighting on the local terrain, ill-equipped and burdened with a conventional military mindset, it was the Indian Army's Vietnam and by the time the IPKF pulled out, it was minus nearly 1,200 men, cremated on a foreign soil and nearly 3,000-plus wounded. In contrast to the Kargil conflict, which was covered extensively by the media, the military entanglement in Sri Lanka is a forgotten war—and was one even while it was being fought—with the last vestiges finally obliterated by the passage of time.

On a trip home on leave from Sri Lanka, I was accosted at the Madras railway station by a few locals asking for donations for their Tamil LTTE brethren. If I hadn't been so noticeably a North Indian, I would have contributed with a punch to their faces, but desisted the urge, fearing a lynching by the locals. Back up north I was asked inane questions by all and sundry if I had managed to get a VCR player and gold. A friend even went as far as to ask me in all earnestness, if I had managed to rape any women.

The novel attempts to capture the life and times of the army, especially the three erstwhile Parachute Commando Units, which were used extensively in the conflict, from start to finish. However, in the narrative, I have used their current nomenclature of Special Forces.

If the Tamil Tigers were such an efficient killing machine, part of the credit should rightly go to the Indian Army. For from 1983 till around 1986, under the direction of the RAW (Research & Analysis Wing), the Indian Army trained around 15,000 Sri Lankan Tamils from various political parties. They were trained in various training establishments spread across the country, with one of the premier ones being Establishment-22 at Chakrata. The school was an American creation, post the 1962 Indo-Chinese war and for a long time was funded by them, to train Tibetan exiles in the art of covert and guerrilla warfare against the Chinese in Tibet. I suspect, my father who was posted there may have perhaps been involved in training the first bunch of Tamil fighters. For certain he was posted at the establishment during the early stages and was more than aware of the happenings there. Little did he know that a few years down the line, his son and his countrymen would be fighting some of the school's ex-students.

When I came back from Sri Lanka and shared the experiences and the losses we had suffered, the old Colonel shocked me by raising a toast to the former students of his ex-organisation.

That the LTTE had extensively entrenched itself in India was public knowledge and not only before, but even during the conflict, the safe houses, cadres and sympathisers active in the country, were never tackled seriously by the Indian government and remained at large, especially in the South Indian states. The Sri Lankan Tamil refugee diaspora in India was of great support, as it was across the world, in financing the Tigers.

In fact, a bizarre postscript to the Sri Lanka episode happened, many years later, just before I left the army in 1998, in Bangalore. The Parachute Training Centre, where I was posted, sent across a South Indian recruit, to help me settle in, as he spoke the language. With a local carpenter's help, I was putting up some paintings. I handed him a small framed Tiger flag, which the unit had presented to all officers who had participated in Operation Pawan in Sri Lanka. The flags were captured in a camp the unit had busted. Needless to say, it was hard-earned and a prized possession. The carpenter had one look at it and went ballistic. He flatly refused to hang it on the wall and an animated conversation in Tamil ensued with the soldier. The South Indian recruit translated it for me.

'It's a Tiger flag,' the recruit explained 'and should not be displayed like this. In fact, he is prepared to buy it.'

'Tell him to bugger off,' I said, 'it's taken blood and sweat to get one of those and it's not for sale.'

The recruit translated my reply to the carpenter and then explained his further comments to me.

'He says that bad things may befall you, Sahib, if you insist on displaying it.'

This was ridiculous; a carpenter was threatening me, in Bangalore, in my own home. So I twisted his arm and snarled into his face that he was a *podiyan*, a Tiger cadre, and I was going to report him to the police. At that he simmered down, but refused to do any more work or accept payment. A day later the flag mysteriously disappeared from the wall and so did the carpenter.

In the end, what could be said about the Tamil Tiger as a fighter? In the history of warfare there would probably be a footnote for the brief time they occupied on the battlefield. But it's the intensity they brought to the fight in that interlude that won them the highest esteem by their adversaries, the Sri Lankan and the Indian Army. With a majority of them looking like undernourished, down-and-out accountants, with no romantic tales of heroism from the past preceding them, they were neither as flamboyant nor as physically impressive as a Pathan mujahidin or an Arab fighter.

But what the Tamil Tigers lacked in looks, they more than made up for in the size of their hearts and could have held their own against the best in the trade. They gave no quarter and asked none, preferring to commit suicide like the Japanese, rather than surrender. As they say: 'It's not the size of the dog in the fight that matters, it's the size of the fight in the dog.' They had two very essential qualities necessary to be formidable in battle—motivation and intelligence—and when unleashed on a terrain of their choice, the results for the enemy were disastrous. No unit that went to the island came back unscathed, for the Tigers busted the myth of the so-called martial races. The motto of the US Special Forces, very aptly sums up the LTTE as a fighting force: *The right man in the right place is a devastating weapon.*

Sketch of Sri Lanka—Northern and Eastern Provinces

Puliyankulam Jungle, Sri Lanka
1988

> *What though the spicy breeze*
> *Blow soft o'er Ceylon's isle*
> *Though every prospect pleases*
> *And only man is vile.*
> —Bishop Reginald Heber, *The Island of Tears*, 1811

The fire lane that cut through the wilderness was wide enough for a small vehicle. Silhouettes of trees stood starkly etched against the clear sky. In the narrow gaps, between the impenetrable foliage above, the firmament was visible, studded with a million sparkling stars. A lone satellite crossed briskly overhead, as if headed for an important errand. Dew and the dank odour of decaying leaves hung heavy over the dark silence; the restlessness of the creatures and the whispers of the wild remained inaudible to the uninitiated. The jungle was quieter than a graveyard after the last mourners had left.

If only the satellite had briefly paused, and its whirring cameras pierced the dense leafy umbrella of the jungle, it would have picked up the presence of alien life in that undergrowth.

Tucked away behind bushes of lantana, lying as still as the trees around, was a fighting patrol of heavily-armed Special Forces (SF) men on a seventy-two-hour ambush operation.

Two pairs of keen young eyes surveyed the path in front with an LMG, a light machine gun covering the prospective killing area. The rest of the troop, split into five-man squads and spread out in a defensive perimeter, waited behind. Captain Hariharan, a.k.a Harry, cast a quick look around, checked his weapon and lay down right behind the two sentries.

Over a period of time, Harry had come to understand exactly how the body and mind behaved during an ambush. For the first few hours, fantasy kept boredom at bay, with daydreams of unleashing an orgy of violence often being strong enough to actually imagine the bullets hitting home. Thirty-six hours down the line, you could hardly bear to eat the rations of puri-sabji, for most of it would have turned stale. After forty-eight hours, you experienced a burning sensation every time you took a leak, signalling the onset of dehydration. All thought now would invariably be about food, water and sleep. Once, Harry had even spent Holi in the bush, when an additional 2-litre can of water that someone had lugged was passed around for a celebratory swig or two as everyone wished each other and shook hands silently.

Water was a huge problem in the jungles of Sri Lanka. Over and above the standard army litre bottle, the men carried extra water in 2-litre jerrycans bought in Madras. The message was clear: if you were stupid enough to sit for days in a bush, then you had to find your own means to survive; the Indian Army had larger issues to worry about. The maps provided were often of World War II vintage, and any *kulam* (ponds) on it had long since dried up on ground. The men also ended up using water for a crap and no amount of coaxing by Harry, to use toilet paper instead, worked, until Harry accidentally discovered the benefits of moist old newspaper. It made excellent toilet paper, saved precious liquid, and so what if it left a bit of the previous day's news on your backside! Of course, there were some old soldiers who could go for days without taking a dump during ambush operations, and Harry was both fascinated and deeply envious of their self-control.

It was their third night out in the wilderness. Harry felt a nudge and opened his eyes to see the sentry on duty uncomfortably close to his face. He could barely make out the blur of stars through the foliage, and as his eyes got used to the dark, he saw Sathish point a finger ahead of them. He concentrated on the track, when he noticed a silhouette right in front of the barrel of the LMG. There was a gentle rise and fall to the dark form and a short grunt like a blocked nose emanated from it. In a whisper, Sathish confirmed Harry's fear: yes, a wild boar, probably high on some fermented fruit. Of all the nooks and corners of the Vanni jungle, the fucker had to choose that spot! If one hadn't used aftershave or hair oil or eaten pickle and raw onions, in thirty-six hours one began to smell of the jungle and became a part of it. Harry was quite pleased; if this guy hadn't smelled their presence yet, then it meant they had passed the jungle warfare test with flying colours. However, the LMG was obstructed and Harry wondered hard how to wake up a snoring boar.

The entire troop was now wide awake and restively fingering their weapons. What if the animal turned around and charged at them? Even a tiger avoids an angry boar. Just a couple of days back, in Mannar, a Jat Battalion soldier had been carried away by an elephant. As if the Tamil Tigers were not enough, now they had to contend with all sorts of wild animals! Worse, what a joke it would be in the unit if he mistook a person for a beast: '*Parlez-vous parlez-vous* of all the animals in the Sri Lankan zoo, the wild boar f...'

Harry's poetic reverie was interrupted when the boar suddenly got up and gave itself a mighty shake. A cloud of dust rose up into the clean night air, and off trotted the boar, grunting as if in complaint. Twenty armed soldiers heaved a collective sigh of relief. 'Thank god!' thought Harry as he tried to see the positive side of the incident, for they were not operating in the Serengeti National Park, where instead of the boar, it could have been a rhino in heat!

Nervous giggles and whispers rippled through the bush as the ambush party readjusted itself and settled down again to the never-ending wait. A little later, a distant throbbing nudged Harry awake. Was the boar coming back with his pals? The sentries stirred. The sound grew louder, and instantly, without a word being exchanged, the men went into battle stations, inching forward to the edge of the thicket, their weapons covering a predefined arc of fire along the length of the path. The throbbing grew louder. Hemmed in by the jungle, the sound rose along the narrow path like a muezzin's call to prayer. Then, in the eyepiece of the night vision device, a small handlebar tractor pulling a trolley lumbered into sight like some miniature prehistoric animal.

Twenty pairs of eyes watched with surging adrenalin as the vehicle slowly rumbled closer. You heard only the slightest of clicks, as down the line, firing levers were pushed to automatic mode and the men, with fingers curled around triggers waited for their leader to give the order to engage. The closeness of the killing area, the volume of fire and the sheer violence of action that would define the moment were all in complete contravention to traditional military teaching. But then this was Sri Lanka, where it was all about improvisation and survival; the Tamil Tigers had turned all textbook-soldiering on its head very early in the conflict. Harry waited, dry-mouthed and with his heart threatening to damage his ribcage, for the tractor to cross the point where a white polythene bag had been tied innocuously to a tree, as the marker for the killing ground. His hands were clammy on the pistol grip, the metal butt of the AK was digging into his shoulder and he could hear Sathish breathing heavily next to him. Time, and his mind, both seemed to have slowed down.

He still hadn't seen any weapons on the men sitting behind in the trolley and was reluctant to pull the trigger. What if they were villagers, women and children? In the fluorescent green night vision, the driver was clearly unarmed, as was the bunch behind, bobbing and swaying sleepily to the motion of the vehicle. The tractor crossed the marker and went past the ambush party and Harry was still reluctant to fire. Then, with an ear-shattering bang, Sathish on his side opened up, clearly following the old dictum, 'When in doubt, empty your magazine'. Within seconds, the rest of the team had joined him, rapidly spewing lead at a phenomenal rate and peppering the target at a mere 10 metres.

The driver was hit immediately and the little tractor wobbled for an instant before it crashed into a tree and overturned. By the time the last echoes subsided, nearly 200 rounds had been fired in thirty seconds. A thin wraith of white smoke hung in the still air, and the sweet smell of cordite was all pervasive. Nothing stirred at the target end and nobody moved at the firing end. Someone let off a nervous single shot, the report loud and incongruous in the aftermath of the volley. Harry cursed softly and demanded to know the name of the soldier. Two men then disengaged from the group and ran down the track to provide cover, while Harry and a few others cautiously approached the vehicle with weapons at the ready and levers switched back to the SF preferred mode of single shot.

There were four men in the trolley, all in a lifeless heap and leaking blood from various holes, like ruptured water pipes. Their weapons lay on the floor of the trolley, slimy with gore. Nanjappa helped himself to a G-3 rifle, while another soldier picked up a Chinese AK, wiping the blood off the weapon on the dead men. Most of the team carried an assortment of captured weapons. Harry noticed that the driver was missing and immediately warned the others. They saw a trail of blood in the faint starlight leading into the jungle. Harry took one look into the dark abyss-like undergrowth and balked at the prospect of tracking a wounded Tiger in that wilderness of entwined roots and bushes. He got on the radio to report briefly to the team commander and then ordered a few men to fire randomly in the general direction where he suspected the wounded Tiger would be lurking. A few bursts later, he hoped they had either got him or that the initial wound would turn fatal and the man, if not already dead, would meet his maker sooner or later.

But the wound was neither fatal nor the man anywhere close to dying. For barely a spitting distance from the edge of the path, curled up behind a tree, and bleeding profusely from a flesh wound lay the driver. Alive, alert and wounded, with the cyanide capsule clenched between his teeth, Silvam listened to the activity in progress on the path. He cursed himself for not having kept his G-3 assault rifle at the ready. He lay there waiting. Soon they would enter the undergrowth and leave him with no choice but to bite into the capsule. Not that Silvam feared death; he had only hoped it would come in battle and not meekly at his own hands. He heard their hushed voices and realised, to his surprise, that they were speaking Haryanvi, a form of Hindi spoken in the north of India. The last time he had heard the language spoken at such close quarters had been around two years before.

'The sister fucker is right in there and can't be very far,' said a voice. 'Doesn't have a weapon either. Should I go after him, sahib?'

'Negative, Sathish, you are not going in there. No hurry, we'll wait for daylight,' answered a more polished voice, authoritative and clearly in command.

Silvam heard radio static and then the man with the polished voice switched to English. 'Alpha two to Alpha one. Over. Contact Alpha one. Confirmed four kills, all hostiles. One injured and probably still lurking somewhere around. Suggest I wait till morning and then wrap him up. Over.'

Silvam was aware there were three Indian Special Forces battalions operating on the island and from the professional manner in which these men were conducting themselves, he was certain this bunch belonged to one of them.

'Orders to move out of the area before there is any retaliation,' called out the officer's voice. 'Booby-trap the bodies and wipe area clean of any footprints and tell-tale signs of our presence.'

'Alright, check equipment and we march in five minutes.'

More conversation followed, and the next thing Silvam heard was the officer give an order to fire in his direction. He barely managed to put his head down, when the undergrowth around him came alive to the whine and angry buzz of hot lead. For a moment, the buzzing sound transported him back to his childhood, when he and his friends had once pulled a beehive down on their way back from school. A cloud of agitated bees had chased them all the way home. Then as suddenly as it had started, it was all over. Like phantoms in the darkness, they were gone. A few bold cicadas now made a brief cry of protest at having been disturbed, and one or two alarmed bats ping-ponged across the starlit clearing in alarm. The denizens of the wild settled down again and a hush descended over the place, as the jungle quickly reverted to its original state of smell and balance.

Silvam was still in shock and couldn't believe it had all actually happened and that his colleagues were lying dead a few feet away. Was it only fifteen minutes back that Mutthu had berated him to drive carefully so they could catch a bit of shut eye? And now he was no more. Slowly he released the cyanide capsule from between his clenched teeth and put it away carefully. He tore a strip from his lungi and tied it around the wound on his arm where the bullet had grazed him. Still bleeding, Silvam floated in and out of consciousness. He thought of his wife and young son, and then his mind drifted to a different time, a different place, far away, where pine trees grew on the mountainside and the Himalayan eagle soared in the cold wind drifts. Just before he fainted, he thought he could actually smell the pine needles, feel them under his feet and hear military commands being given, not in his mother tongue Tamil but, strangely, in the language of his enemy: Hindi.

After collecting the weapons and placing a grenade under one of the bodies, the ambush party left the scene like a bunch of guilty school boys who had raided an apple orchard. Within minutes they were swallowed by the night, leaving no signs to reveal the perpetrators of the deed, except for hundreds of spent shells on the jungle floor. Harry cut cross-country for a few miles before going into a commando harbour for the few hours of darkness. At first light, they set out again and were still not out of the jungle when they heard machine-gun fire at close quarters. Experienced hands recognised it as from a fellow battalion, judging from the sound and the pattern of twenty-round bursts.

They emerged on the main road and saw a road opening party (ROP) of Sikh troops crawling along from the Vavuniya end like a *baraat* (marriage procession) gone sour. A burly Sikh manned an MMG, a medium machine gun mounted on top of a vehicle, which he swung at random and unleashed a burst or two into the bushes on either side—speculative fire, which was a safer way to discourage an ambush. Soldiers walked alongside and ahead of the vehicles, with a couple of them carrying metal detectors and one of them leading an obese, unhappy black Labrador, his tongue hanging halfway to the ground, panting rapidly to cool itself in the muggy heat.

Harry exchanged a look with the others at the close call. Had they been a little ahead, the lead would have been coming their way. If there was anything more accurate than incoming enemy fire, it was incoming friendly fire. At first, the Sikhs looked somewhat surprised to see a body of men emerge from the bush, all armed to the teeth and bearded to the eyes. Perhaps they thought a bunch of Sikhs had gone rogue. The MMG swung menacingly to cover them momentarily; then it was all bonhomie and the team got a lift halfway till the Jat Battalion post where they were attached for operations. The lead vehicle had a few local women seated on it, with or without their consent, Harry was not sure. They sat quietly on the floor, avoiding any eye contact with the men. Harry thought it made sense to have the locals, especially women, ride along as protection against a possible IED (improvised explosive device) attack. One would, after all, think twice before blowing up one's own kith and kin and if one had to cart the locals along, then rather the fairer sex—sensible Sikh logic.

A little ahead at the midway point, they ran into the Jat ROP. Harry took in the scene. It was around ten in the morning. The temperature was rising and humidity hung heavy like an unseen blanket, enervating and irritating. The bushes on either side of the road were ablaze, crackling from time to time when they received a fresh gust of breeze. The heat could be felt on the road and the smoke stung the eyes. A few soldiers and civilians were scurrying ahead with burning torches and setting every dry twig afire. An NCO (Non-commissioned officer) stood with a cloth wrapped around his head like a turban, wielding a rifle like a staff. At his feet squatted an abject local, holding his ears in what they called the *murga* or rooster position back at the Military Academy. Under a bare tree, a soot-blackened pot sat atop a makeshift stone stove, its lid gently murmuring as the water boiled inside. A radio set lay in a heap next to it.

The NCO was one of those quintessential Jats, big, brawny, cropped hair with cat's eyes and devilment written all over his face. One look at the unusual colour of the eyes on his swarthy Indian face, and Harry couldn't help wondering if Alexander and his band of merry Greeks hadn't hunkered down for R&R (Rest and Recoup) in his village in Haryana long long ago. The staff became a rifle again as the NCO saw an officer approaching. Offering Harry a cup of sweet tea, he told him that they were clearing the undergrowth with fire. Apparently, they had lost a few men in an ambush on the same stretch; now it was a policy of fire and fire, he grinned, pointing at the fire and at his rifle. 'No bush sahib, no ambush,' he declared, pausing to poke the local, who had slackened his position, with his barrel.

The Jat seemed a friendly, chatty sort. A radio operator, his office was adjacent to Harry's room. 'Do you know,' he joked as they walked up to the post, 'that the Jats worshipped the monkey god Hanuman and so it was the second time in history that someone was burning Lanka a la Hanumanji!' His name was Satbir, and he had been on the island for over a year. They walked back to the post with Satbir regaling Harry with all the incidents that had happened in their area of operation, pointing out landmarks and spots where an ambush or a firefight had taken place. He was full of praise for his Company Commander Captain Sudhir, and Harry was looking forward to catching up with him as they had been coursemates.

Clearly, Sudhir seemed to have the environment under control and was thinking out of the box to stay ahead of the Liberation Tigers of Tamil Eelam (LTTE) in the game.

The next morning, Harry was woken up by the choicest abuses in Haryanvi. Peeking through a hole in the wooden partition, Harry saw Satbir frothing at the mouth. A thin foreign voice rang loud and clear over the radio, speaking in broken Hindi and English: 'Indian dogs, sister fuckers, you will go back. Step out of your post,' and so on. At this, the Greek from Haryana went ballistic, challenging him to personal combat and threatening to fuck anything Sri Lankan on two legs, regardless of sex or age: 'And just you wait, in a few years there will be half-a-dozen half-breed children running around and one of them will be your whore sister's!'

The Jat's buddy, another potential descendant of Alexander's lost army, chuckled and prompted him to convey that if it was a boy they could name him Satbir in the father's memory and if it was a girl…er, well…then just call her a whore. All very satisfying to let off steam, but Harry doubted the Tamil Tiger had understood a word. Post commander Sudhir later informed Harry that this was a regular conversation Satbir had with the unidentified Tiger station and the evening powwow between the two was generally quite polite. Presently, another voice broke in. It was distinctly nasal and high-pitched and seemed tired and in pain. Harry quickly summoned Sathish who was a South Indian and spoke Tamil.

To everyone's amazement, the new voice spoke fluent Hindi with just the slightest trace of an accent. He warned the Indian radio operator to mind his language, then announced the name of the battalion and the location and threatened to personally come and teach the Jats a lesson. For a moment, Harry thought he had heard the voice somewhere, then, considering the circumstances, dismissed the idea just as promptly. Thereafter the conversation continued between the two Tigers in staccato bursts and Sathish had to strain to decipher their accent.

When the radio chat came to an end, Sathish nodded unhappily at Harry. 'You should have allowed me to go after the guy in the bush,' he said. 'That was him, reporting the incident and confirming he was shot. He has managed to reach one of the camps, and he is certain the ambush was carried out by an SF team. He is talking about retaliation now.'

Kumulamunai to Chakrata

*I have tried caution and forethought; from now on
I shall make myself mad*

—Rumi

Silvam was born in Kumulamunai, a small village close to the Nayaru Lagoon. His birth name was Sivashankar Kumaran and he was born in the year when Sri Lanka's giant neighbour India was dealt a shocking defeat by the Chinese in a war along its north-eastern border, and when Tamil politicians in his country were mooting the idea of a separate nation. It was the winter of 1962. The core problem of Sri Lanka—that of identity—was slowly metamorphosing into a movement where the Tamils wanted to preserve their identity, while the Sinhalas wanted to crush it. His father was a teacher at the village primary school and like most Tamil parents his emphasis was on education and his dream was to see his only son work in a stable firm or for the government in a big city. It was a time when Sinhala chauvinism and jingoistic fervour were on a high and 'good' jobs were reserved for Sinhalas, with Tamils being treated as second-class citizens.

That was a sore point, which irked the educated Tamil population of the country and often veered the general conversation at home towards the deteriorating Tamil–Sinhala politics. The young boy's personality was shaped in this all-pervasive atmosphere of mistrust and hatred. Born with one leg shorter than the other, Shiva, as he was called, walked with a limp and as a consequence, often got relegated to the position of an onlooker in any game or physical activity throughout his school life. Stout, because of a lack of exercise and hampered by a prominent limp, he was savagely ridiculed by other children in school, as they are often wont to do. But what he lacked physically, he more than made up for mentally. Withdrawn and quiet to the point of being taciturn, Shiva was a thinker, with dreams of doing big things and being recognised.

Shiva was fifteen when he first heard the name of Prabhakaran. The Tamil community was agog with tales of his daring exploits and the party he had formed—LTTE. However, these were early days of Tamil resistance and the movement had yet to gain a coherent direction. Various parties were coming to the fore and vying for political authority, both with the Tamil population and the Sri Lankan government. Shiva finished his education at the village school and got admission at Jaffna University to study accounting. He was a bright and a hardworking student, with a mind made for enquiry. When he was not studying accounts, Shiva could often be found sitting under a tree reading poetry.

The university campus was rife with student unions which were aligned to various parties and active in local politics. However, none approached Shiva considering his reticent nature and possibly his noticeable handicap. He finished college and found a job in the accounts department of a small company exporting fish and spices. Its office was in the main Jaffna market and he found himself a room on rent in the suburbs at Kokkuvil, 10 kilometres away. Shiva, true to his nature, was a sincere worker, arriving on time after cycling the long distance to office and would often stay back late after official work hours. He was acutely aware of the sacrifices his father had made to give him a good education and he wanted to give his parents the best in their old age.

However, sometimes the best-laid plans of man are thwarted by the gods, for they have larger events in mind. Events, which decide the destiny of a people and a nation, when mere mortals are often sucked into the maelstrom, to be carried along like an insignificant twig. Such events were unfolding and gathering momentum just then and were often reflected in the violence that erupted from time to time between the Sinhalas and the repressed Tamil population. Shiva could sense the hostility in his workplace. While his performance and efforts were way better than his three Sinhala colleagues, the end-of-the-year appraisal saw them going home with more bonuses and salary hikes. The message was clear—this is Sinhala country and you are a second-class minority.

Shiva thought briefly of trying his fortunes in the Middle East, but his father was not in good health and he was the only child. On one of his trips home, he was married off to his neighbour's daughter who had been his junior in school. She was a vivacious, pretty eighteen-year-old and Shiva, a serious, brooding twenty-two. He took his young wife Laxmi back to Jaffna, where she quickly took charge of their one-bedroom home. The spartan room was soon converted into a bright little place, with plastic flowers and posters of gods benevolently looking down from the walls. But if there was domestic peace within for Shiva, it was matched with an equal measure of turmoil without. For north-east Sri Lanka was on a boil, erupting into an unimaginable orgy of violence. The situation in Jaffna was rapidly deteriorating and Shiva thought it best to pack his wife back to his parents' house. Laxmi had never looked prettier, as she was glowing with their child in her womb. The year was 1984.

Laxmi had barely left, when suddenly all semblance of normality crumbled and the disaster that struck Shiva changed the course of his life forever. If he had the slightest inkling that he was walking down a one-way street, which ended in a cul-de-sac, he would have altered course. But how was he to know?

On a blistering hot day, when he came back from office, he found his father-in-law waiting for him at his house. The news was devastating. Both his parents had been killed by Sri Lankan security forces in a cordon and search operation. They had fired at his father and when his mother had tried to snatch the weapon away she had been shot too. The charges against them were all trumped-up. This was an all-too-familiar scenario with the security forces, when they were instructed to carry out ethnic cleansing. The army was now looking for him. 'Go to India,' his father-in-law urged, 'and once you have settled down, we will follow with Laxmi and the child.'

The rickety fishing boat designed to carry ten people was crammed with double the number, along with all the meagre belongings each of them could carry. They crossed the Palk Strait where a summer storm was lashing the gunwale with ferocious waves and threatening to capsize them at any moment. Shiva sat through the journey, impervious to the discomfort or the possibility of death, for he was too grief-stricken to bother. They came ashore at Rameshwaram and he found himself following the hundreds of people making their way to the refugee camps. He felt lost and sad and a profound loneliness sat heavy in his heart. But his was not a character to sit idle and wallow in self-pity for too long. He soon volunteered to join the skeleton administration team running the camp and helped them with documentation and the rudimentary accounting they needed.

Barely a week into his new life, he was approached by a few men. They introduced themselves as members of the LTTE and asked him point blank if he would be interested in joining.

'What do I have to do if I join?' asked Shiva. He had heard of the group, of course, and was a silent admirer of Prabhakaran, the leader of the party.

'Fight for Eelam,' was the curt reply.

Within a day or two, Shiva found himself a part of a group of twenty young men, all hand-picked by the Tamil Tigers from across the refugee camps. While they were all different in age and temperament, they had, however, one thing in common. All of them had lost at least one close family member to the Sri Lankan forces and were, therefore, bound by a mutual feeling of revenge. Soon they were kitted out and escorted to the railway station by a bunch of new men, all clearly South Indians. The LTTE leader had one last word with each of them, ticked something on a cardboard file and handed him over to the Indians. He looked at Shiva disparagingly for some time, clearly showing his hesitation at the selection. Then suddenly making up his mind, he whispered, 'Your name now is Silvam. Remember it, for you will take this name to your grave. You will dedicate yourself to the cause and sever all ties with your past life, including your family. Hope you are not married,' he continued, 'for the leader has banned matrimony.'

'No, not at all,' replied Shiva in some confusion.

'Good then. Remember you have been picked up more for your brain then your body. Learn well what the Indians have to teach and don't let that handicap of yours come in the way. Godspeed, Silvam.'

The group, closely chaperoned by the Indians, was led to a separate train compartment at the far end of the platform and kept apart from other passengers. A little later, the wheels clattered and clanked, bogeys jostled each other as if in mock delight and with a final jerk, the train pulled out of the station. A shiver of excitement ran through Silvam, for he was embarking on an unknown adventure in a foreign country. The group was received by a different set of people at the Delhi railway station and transported to a large house in a very normal-looking residential colony. There Silvam found the food, though different, was good and rooms comfortable. However, when he tried to go outside for a bit of fresh air, one of their handlers, dressed in plain clothes, stationed outside the apartment, stopped him.

Two days later, after some more documentation and background screening had been conducted by the Indians, the group was again loaded, this time onto a large Tata bus, with curtains pulled across the windows. At the crack of dawn, while the city still slept, the bus drove down the Ring Road, heading out of the city and turned northwards. While most of his companions immediately fell asleep, Silvam peered out through a crack in the curtain at the North Indian countryside slipping by. He observed the signboards and read their names with ease as most of them were in English and guessed they were heading north. The sun rose, the heat increased and with every hour the terrain changed. Five hours later, Silvam saw the mountains before him and shortly after crossing a river at the foothills, the bus wound its way up a narrow road. When they finally alighted, the heat and dust had been left behind, the weather was brisk and the surroundings sublime. The hill station was called Chakrata and Silvam just loved the place.

India
1984

You don't become a guerrilla on a full stomach.
—Col Silvam, LTTE

The river Yamuna running its course through the mountains, finally debouches itself in the plains at a place called Dakpathar. The fury of the river here is contained by a dam. A narrow road crosses the river at this point. Going past the second-century Mauryan rock edict at Kalsi, it winds its way up the mountain into an area known as Jaunsar-Bawar. The locals believe that the Pandavas in their journey to the mountains went through their country and following their tradition, the local Jaunsaris were a matriarchal society, practising polyandry. Clinging to the treacherous mountainside, often prone to landslides, the road finally climbs up to nearly 7,000 feet through forests of conifer, oak and rhododendrons to the small hill station of Chakrata. Established as a cantonment town, in the latter half of the nineteenth century by the British, the town and its environs hardly developed over the years and the single road remained a one-way route, with fixed timings being adhered to for traffic going up or coming down. Entry for outsiders into the area was regulated with check posts and permits.

If development had bypassed Jaunsar, it was not by default, but by design. For the Indian Army ran a top-secret training base here called the Establishment 22 (called Two Two). The establishment was started primarily to train Tibetan refugees in guerrilla warfare, which they would then carry out in Chinese-occupied Tibet. Sturdy-looking Khampa tribesmen could be seen climbing rocks, firing weapons and going out for their morning runs. Over time it became a mini-Tibetan town, with the Mongoloid-looking hill men in complete consonance with the mountains around. No one gave them a second look. From time to time, the facility—diverting from its original task of churning out Tibetan saboteurs—was also used for training operatives, from various parts of the subcontinent, who were sent by the intelligence agencies to learn how to carry out unsavoury tasks that are sometimes required to achieve political ends.

Therefore the arrival in station, in the early 1980s, of a group of dark, frail-looking men of South Indian origin, raised no flutter amongst the locals or from the Indian Army instructors. Accustomed to not asking any questions, they designed the training as per the brief received and assumed, that like the other non-Tibetans who turned up for training, these men would also disappear from their lives soon. But by 1984, regular batches of these dark men were graduating from the school, learning a curriculum in violence. Led by a tall aristocratic-looking Colonel from the Paratroops, the Indian trainers kept their wards busy, teaching them a tradecraft which would help them to stay alive in a volatile environment and spread mayhem.

The three-month training schedule was unforgiving—physicals, weapon handling and explosive training in the mornings were followed by theory classes on guerrilla warfare in the afternoons. While there were a number of camps, mostly in Tamil Nadu, the most secretive was the Two Two Establishment, and the initial lot of the LTTE were trained here. If there was anything that bothered Silvam and his colleagues in this strange mountain abode, it was the cold and the food. While they soon got accustomed to the cold, they just couldn't digest the North Indian fare of dal and roti and pined for spicy fish curry and rice.

Silvam, with his superior intellect, very quickly learned Hindi and with a smattering of English already under his belt, he soon came to the notice of the Indian instructors. They also discovered that his portly frame and limp were no handicap when it came to physical work, for while he was a poor runner, he more than made up for it when it came to long-route marches. Apart from being educated, his pluck and drive soon earned him the admiration of his instructors. They elevated him as the group leader and referred to him for any advice they needed with regard to the training and welfare of the students. Silvam revelled in their attention, for he was finally getting the recognition he had always dreamt of. But what Silvam found difficult to swallow was the disdain some of the North Indian instructors had for their fighting ability. Referring to them as Madrasis, the instructors could be harsh and humiliating in their language. It only made Silvam more determined to prove to their detractors how wrong they were. An idli-dosa eating man could be a match to any fighter. Little did he know that his wish would soon be granted and against the very men who doubted their martial qualities.

At no stage during the students' stay at the school were they allowed out of the heavily-guarded complex, not that there was much to do in the small cantonment town. The only exception to this rule was Silvam. Representing the course as their leader and with a list of things to be bought, from slippers to South Indian spices and condiments, he would regularly go down with the rations vehicle to the nearest big city—Dehradun. The Colonel, on these weekend runs, would often go along, hitching a ride in the bus to Dehradun, where he had built a house in anticipation of his forthcoming retirement.

On a bitterly cold December morning, a civilian bus stopped in front of a house in Vasant Vihar, a retired officers' colony in Dehradun. The curtains had been drawn on every window of the bus and nothing of the inside was visible. Only the driver could be seen through the windscreen. Though the driver was wearing civilian clothes, the stamp of a soldier was unmistakable from the cut of his face. The Colonel got down followed by a short, plump, dark man of South Indian origin, with a pronounced limp, carrying his overnight suitcase. Harry, the Colonel's son and himself an army officer, was back on leave after finishing his combat diving course with the navy and was relaxing in the verandah reading the newspaper. The man deposited the suitcase in the verandah and wished Harry a polite 'Morning *Saar*'. The Colonel introduced him as their new canteen contractor, who came down quite often to Doon to collect supplies. The man had a glass of water and then touched the Colonel's feet and took his leave.

Harry was on a month's annual leave and for the next four weeks, he ran into Silvam every time the Colonel came down to spend the weekend with his family. On each occasion the drill was the same. Deposit the suitcase, wish Harry, have a glass of water and then before departing, touch the Colonel's feet. Harry found it rather strange and accosted his father about it.

'How come a canteen contractor gives you such respect? And since when have you allowed people to touch your feet? We have never done it and it is not followed in the family either.'

'Oh! Silvam,' quipped the Colonel, 'he has suffered some huge financial and personal losses. He is a good man, so I gave him the contract. Seems to be eternally grateful for it. I have told him so many times that touching feet should be reserved only for your parents and the gods. Nobody else deserves it.'

Only on one occasion, the day before Harry was finishing his leave and heading back to join his unit in the hills did Silvam agree to sit down, as he waited for the Colonel to finish his packing. Keeping to his taciturn nature or following the Colonel's orders, he remained tight-lipped and reserved. But in the brief conversation they had, Harry understood two things very clearly. One, Silvam had no idea about running a canteen and was vague in the odd question thrown at him regarding his business. And two, he had great respect and affection for some of the officers and men in the school, especially for the Colonel.

A few months later, the Colonel retired and hung up his uniform and the canteen contractor with the limp disappeared from his life forever. Much later *India Today* carried an article on the rise of the LTTE and India's hand in training and equipping the guerrilla force. Chakrata figured in the list of the locations where training was conducted. Back home on a short spell of leave, Harry cornered his father and inquired about the canteen contractor. The Colonel had retired by then and the information he had was in the public domain in any case, so he felt no reason to deny his son's assertion.

'Yes, the contractor was a Sri Lankan Tamil,' he said, 'and belonged to one of the many political parties, I think it was the LTTE. Raw kids when they arrived, some hadn't even worn a shoe in their life and they were definitely not fighting material. But when we worked out their training schedule,' continued the Colonel, 'their leader approached us—the man you met—and requested, if instead of a nine-hour schedule, could it be increased to thirteen. I'd like to believe, we made something of a soldier out of each of them. They should give a good account of themselves against the Sri Lankan army. They had something very necessary for a fighting man, my boy. They had tons and tons of motivation. In fact,' and the Colonel looked Harry in the eye, 'some of them were good enough for my own unit.' A high compliment from the Colonel, who carried the belief that the Parachute Unit he had served in, was God's own gift to soldiering.

⊕

Silvam ended up staying for a year at Chakrata at the behest of the Indian instructors. He was a great help in bridging the gap between the students and the teachers. Sometime in early 1986, he was sent back and made his way to Jaffna. A full-fledged war was on with the Sri Lankan army and the LTTE was the dominant party, leading the fight. Silvam with his unassuming scholarly looks which belied the fire in him, joined the war with gusto. It was as if he was born to be a warrior, or perhaps his longer stay in Chakrata had prepared him better for combat. He was calm under fire and had a natural instinct for unconventional, guerrilla warfare. The higher-ups in the hierarchy of the party were watching and earmarking him for greater responsibility.

He was given command of a ten-man unit and entrusted with the task of preparing the defences around Jaffna city. Being an educated man, his grasp of explosives was better than most and he had a knack of selecting the most suitable place for IEDs and mines, unlike the others, who often got the calculations wrong and had a general tendency to overdo the explosive content. The Sri Lankan offensive to capture the city of Jaffna was expected to resume any time and all roads and by-lanes leading into the city from the south had to be defended. Morale in the ranks was high, the general population supportive and the best the Sri Lankans could throw at them, had made not a dent in the LTTE's military machine, for their fighting prowess remained unmatched. Of course, they were surreptitiously helped all along by Big Brother India. Physically the country was already carved out, for the LTTE governed the occupied areas and it was only a matter of time before exhaustion of resources, man and material, compelled the Sri Lankan government to secede to their demands, for an independent Eelam.

Then sometime in early 1987, the long-standing status quo was disturbed by the entry most unexpectedly, of a third stakeholder in the struggle. The Indians entered the fray. First, only as observers, sitting peacefully at the Palaly airfield, silently watching from the sidelines, how their old students conducted themselves against a conventional army. Sometime later, with bated breath, everyone watched the outcome of the big political powwow happening in far-off Delhi.

The decisions that were taken soon unfolded events on the ground, the ramifications of which left great grief on either side of the Palk Strait. For the peaceful watchers at the Palaly airfield were languorously stirring themselves. The great Indian military juggernaut was on the roll and not as the LTTE had always hoped, in their support, but much to their disappointment and chagrin, against them.

The Tigers fought like demented dervishes high on hashish and the Indians had to battle for every inch of ground to capture Jaffna. The LTTE planning had been meticulous and the defences prepared during peacetime to hold good against the Sri Lankans, were now paying off rich dividends against the Indian assault. Every street corner had been turned into a veritable fortress with roadblocks and sandbag walls to be contested in blood. Very soon, to break the impasse, Indian tanks and BMP armoured personnel carriers made their appearance in support of their beleaguered infantry. Silvam was in the thick of battle with his team as a mobile reserve force, bolstering roadblock units, where reinforcements were required.

On numerous occasions, he had a close brush with death, always coming away unscathed and surprised at his fortune, for the battle was intense and unforgiving. On one occasion, while he was trying to engage a tank with a rocket-propelled grenade launcher (RPG), it turned and fired its main gun at point blank range. The house they were using for cover in the street fight collapsed and both his colleagues were killed. Unconscious, he woke up after a few hours, surprisingly unhurt, except for a splitting headache. The street had been taken, for he heard Indian voices and through the fallen debris saw Gurkha soldiers marching past. He waited for nightfall and then undeterred made his way back to the LTTE lines, which he noticed had shrunk considerably.

Jaffna was a lost cause for certain and some of the cadres were instructed to break contact and head towards the jungle camps and other towns further south. Silvam was ordered to report to the tactical headquarters at the university campus, where all the senior LTTE commanders were gathering for a war council, to be presided over by none other than Prabhakaran. By midday a large gathering of the LTTE's commanders and rank and file, belligerent to a man and bristling with weapons, had converged on to the sprawling campus. Before the briefing could commence, confirmed intelligence came in of an impending Indian raid, the objective of which was lost on no one; to capture or kill the LTTE's senior leadership and bring the conflict to an early end.

The choices with Prabhakaran were limited to only two. Instruct the cadres to disperse and melt away, leaving the area empty for the Indians to look like fools, or lay out a warm reception. The Tamil leader didn't have to contemplate too long on such options. He hadn't become the founder and the leader of one of the finest guerrilla outfits in the world by shying away from hard decisions or from a good fight. He decided to stay put and give the Indians a bloody nose. Suddenly, the purpose of the gathering, from a council of war, had altered to the conduct of one at its doorstep. The preparations were hasty but adequate and the Tigers waited for the brewing storm to break.

Silvam was on the roof of the main building block when the first helicopter was heard approaching. The .50 calibre machine guns and the deployment of the men had been done facing towards the sea in anticipation of the expected line of flight. However, taking off from the Palaly airfield, a mere four minutes flying time to the target, the Indians approached from the opposite side. In the blackness of the October night, with even the tail light switched off, the first MI-8 chopper managed to disgorge its human cargo and take off before any accurate fire could be directed at it. Within minutes the next one arrived, landing in a swirling cloud of dust in the football field in front of the LTTE stronghold.

Silvam and the others had by then hopped across to the other end of the roof and were blazing away in the darkness, more in the general direction of the sound as nothing was visible. More choppers were heard approaching, but by then the Tigers had got an idea of the flight path and the landing zone. In spite of the fire being devastatingly accurate, strangely none of the choppers exploded into a ball of fire as Silvam had expected. Unbeknownst to the LTTE fighters, the firing had been extremely effective and most of the helicopters which had tried to land, had been severely damaged, barely managing to limp the short trip home.

Silvam wondered if anyone had managed to get out of the choppers, for the firing was withering and the choppers too had hardly spent any time on the ground. He admired the pilots for their courage to be flying blind into a raging inferno of lead. Then the first tiny flash of light appeared from the periphery of the field, to be joined shortly by many more pops, as the Indian tracers started crossing paths with the Tigers' fire. Silvam had his answer, the Indian Army had arrived, but in what numbers was difficult to guess, judging purely from the incoming fire.

In spite of their surprise getting compromised and the raiding force walking into a well-laid out ambush, Silvam found the agility and aggression of the Indians in such trying circumstances admirable. They had bounced back very fast and were trying to regain the lost initiative. Some of them were advancing rapidly towards the buildings and Prabhakaran wisely decided to make himself scarce. Sometime during the night he left the premises, issuing orders to continue the battle. The morning brought no solace to the Indians, for the planned brigade link-up was nowhere in sight. The advance had stalled somewhere on the outskirts of the city.

Silvam was present at the final annihilation of the Sikh troops, when they were completely exposed in broad daylight and without any cover in the open field. The last of the Sikhs made a courageous bayonet charge. But it was a perfunctory gesture by a race of men known for their sheer audacity in battle. Twenty-nine were killed and only one man survived to tell the tale. The other troops with the Sikhs had however disappeared during the hours of darkness. Holed up in two houses, they were now giving it back to the Tigers and would continue to do so for the next eighteen hours. It was as fine a rearguard action as any and for Silvam, it was his first experience of the Indian Special Forces. His respect for them grew enormously and would remain so till the end of his days. Little did he know that their paths would cross often, violently, leaving a trail of blood in its wake.

Jaffna slipped out of the LTTE's grasp and so did the rest

of the so-called Eelam country. The remnants of the Tigers silently melted away into the jungles and Silvam joined them to continue the fight. He was, by any reckoning, a seasoned fighter, having fought against both the Indian and the Sri Lankan military and if he had been a member of a regular army, they would have decorated him a few times by then, for conspicuous gallantry in action.

⊕

Sri Lanka
1988

People join us not because we are different,
But because, they are.
—Special Forces saying

While Harry was ploughing through his mandatory Young Officers course at Mhow, his unit had been flown in to Sri Lanka. The ink on the Indo-Sri Lanka accord had barely dried when hostilities broke out and a contingent of the Indian Army, euphemistically called the Indian Peace Keeping Force, IPKF, was thrown in to enforce the law and in doing so, got embroiled in a vicious war. Harry was keeping a close watch on the happenings on the island. The unit had taken casualties very early in the conflict and Harry was chaffing at the bit to join them, quite unable to focus on his studies. The moment he finished the last exam, he was off like a shot.

A twenty-two-hour journey and Harry landed in Madras. A liaison detachment from the unit got in touch and informed him that he needed to get across ASAP. Harry couldn't understand the hurry, after all one Lieutenant was not going to change the course of events if he turned up a day or two late. The military flights were all chock-a-block, so Harry was booked on a ship due to sail the next day. The MV Akbar was on the Mecca route, when it was commandeered by the army for troop movement. Designed for people who could pay well to travel in comfort, the Akbar was definitely a superior ship to sail in, as compared to most naval vessels. Harry spent most of his time between lying on the bunk and trips on the deck to get some fresh air, basically to get his nausea under control. As a combat diver, with nearly 200 hours of dive time under his belt, he was more comfortable under water, than sailing on the surface. The ship took more than the usual thirty-six hours to cross the Palk Strait, but finally on the third day they sighted the island of Sri Lanka.

Harry shut the book he had been reading on the history of the island and went up to the deck. From a distance, in the grey dawn light, only a strip of green was visible, with tiny palm trees breaking above the foliage. Looking at the thin wedge of land, it was difficult to imagine that a huge land mass extended beyond. Gradually the strip broadened, to unveil signs of human habitation and the palm trees came alive to the gentle breeze blowing inland from the sea. Harry wondered about this ancient land, its name familiar to every Hindu from childhood, the country of king Ravana and an island invaded by Lord Rama.

Over the centuries the island was known by many names and one of the earliest came from some of the Ashokan rock edicts, where the name Tambapanni is mentioned. The Ramayana which predates the Mauryan period and was written perhaps 2,500 years ago, mentions the current name of Lanka.

When the Portuguese took over Jaffna from the resident Sinhala, they named the place Ceilao. The Dutch East India Company were the next to arrive, driving the Portuguese out in 1658, followed by the British who arrived in 1796 and promptly anglicised Ceilao to Ceylon.

There was a time when the island was joined to the Indian subcontinent by a thin strip of land mass and then around the end of the Ice Age, the sea level rose and the water severed the connection. But Harry was more interested in the recent history of Sri Lanka—the first armed landing which had been carried out in 1795-96 by the British to capture the various port cities. The Madras Presidency, being the closest, provided the expeditionary force to capture the three port cities of Trincomalee, Batticaloa and Jaffna. Harry's battalion, raised in the Carnatic, formed a part of the invading force that landed in Ceylon sometime in 1796. It struck Harry that the second time the unit landed on the island was after nearly two centuries, in 1987. He had gone through the Digest of Service and there was no mention of the casualties the force suffered then, but he was certain the butchers' bill was much higher in 1987, with three Captains dead and another five wounded and the game was still in play, indeed it had just begun.

As the ship anchored at the Trincomalee harbour, feverish activity exploded on the docks. Military vehicles pulled out honking, whistles blew and everything below was a mass of moving olive green, for there were no civilians to be seen. A soldier next to Harry was hauling some large bundles wrapped in cloth and the moment the ship came alongside the quay, he hurled one below. A tall Sikh was waiting for it and promptly loaded it into a vehicle. The man tossed another bundle down, which landed with a thud on the quay and split open scattering colourful Madras check lungis all around. A Military Police Sergeant noticed and walked across. The last Harry saw, as he got into the jeep sent to collect him, was the three of them huddled in a parley. 'Lots of demand for Indian lungis,' Harry's driver told him as they drove away. Clearly the army had been around long enough to start dabbling in local business.

Harry drove along a beautiful gently winding road with clear blue sea on one side and dark green vegetation from across the road throwing shadows on the placid water. In a few months it was going to get humid, but in January at that time the weather was balmy. The city of Trincomalee was built on a peninsula, which divided the inner and the outer harbours overlooking the Kottiyar Bay. The beauty of Trinco belied the violence lurking in the unseen shadows and it was difficult to attribute the tales of death and destruction that Harry had been hearing about the place.

Trinco was one of the finest natural deep harbours and post the fall of Singapore was the home of the Eastern fleet and the South-Eastern command under Lord Mountbatten during World War II. Harry drove past huge fuel tanks built by the British during the war, standing like giant old sentinels, dominating the bay and in spite of repeated attempts by the Tigers to wrest control of the place, a small enclave around the harbour remained throughout with the government forces. The battalion's base was on a jetty and consisted of a few cottages. The Adjutant who had been shot in the hand and had volunteered to get back to the island, greeted Harry warmly and informed him he would be heading off to join Bravo Team.

A chopper and a truck ride later, Harry reported to the team at Mankulam. A senior Captain and two Majors sat drinking rum and playing scrabble. The quarters were in tents and the team was attached to a J&K Battalion. That night there was a massive amount of firing, with tracers stitching patterns above them in the sky. Knowing how trigger-happy the Indians were, the Tigers would often send jitter parties to spook the posts into blowing up ammo.

'Your welcome reception,' Major Sharma, the team commander smilingly told Harry. However, the fireworks didn't seem to bother the officers, as they continued with their drinking and scrabble in the lamplight. They brought him up to speed on recent happenings and most of the conversation was about death and casualties. Later in the evening, Harry got a radio message from a friend informing him about losing a coursemate Rajesh Kumar in a rocket attack. Harry was distraught, after hearing the news. Not only coursemates, Rajesh and Harry were from the same platoon and company in the Academy. Harry got the impression that on an average, the army was losing a man a day. The violence levels were high and there was no time for a gradual introduction into operations. The very next day Harry took charge of 'Seven Troop' and hit the jungle for a seek-and-destroy mission. This was the army's hard school. You learn on the job, learn quick or cease to exist.

After the initial clash with the much larger Indian Army, the LTTE very wisely withdrew from the urban centres and disappeared into their jungle lairs, to operate as a ghost force, striking at will at the omnipresent Indian Army. Flying in and out of Mankulam on a regular basis, the operations continued at a feverish pace and Seven Troop was thrown around all over the island, for area domination, or in a firefighting role, wherever a local unit had been mauled by the Tigers. The modus operandi on such occasions remained the same; load up and disappear into the jungle for thirty-six to seventy-two-hour ops. The team had fallen in and Harry was waiting to give his report, a quick summary of the patrol strength, arms and equipment and the means of communication to be followed, before stepping out on one of the usual seek-and-destroy missions.

A mess waiter walked up with a glass of neat rum on a tray, with Captain's epaulets dipped in the glass, soaking in the spirit. Harry knew the drill. In one huge swig he drained the glass, the liquid tearing a fiery path down his throat. He hauled out the cloth epaulets with his teeth. The team commander and the senior JCO (Junior Commissioned Officer) then rolled them up on his shoulder. The men clapped, shook hands and the young Captain gave the command for the team to roll out of the post. The rest of the day, Harry was belching rum fumes and felt light-headed and woozy. He only hoped that the Tamil Tigers were not familiar with the smell of the Indian Army rum, for he was sure the stench would dominate all other smells in the bush. It was a short twenty-four-hour jaunt in the jungle, and the next day Harry decided to roll back to camp. On the way, he got a message to check out a few huts in a small hamlet where some hostile movement had been reported.

A couple of dilapidated huts were quickly cordoned. The place looked devoid of human presence and was rather quiet. As Harry cautiously walked towards the huts, a few children of varying sizes, peered and sized him up, from behind clothes and sheets which were hanging outside to dry. There was a sudden movement from behind one of the sheets, and an emaciated man tried to flee. He was brought down immediately and Harry questioned him as his children watched in utter shock. The kids were so taken with the violence that they forgot to cry and stood clutching each other for courage, watching their father get battered. Then the youngest started to whimper and Harry knew it was just a matter of time before the whole lot of them would have joined the Ceylon crying chorus. Harry didn't like doing it in front of the kids, so they dragged the man into the nearest hut.

It was a barren mud and thatch hovel, with a poster of a familiar-looking god on one wall with a few utensils stacked on a shelf below it. In the gloom, Harry saw two women in one corner of the hut. One of them was clearly in the throes of advanced labour, while the other was kneeling next to her uttering encouragement and instructions. Perhaps, she was a local midwife or a relative. The pregnant woman was pinching her lips to control herself from crying aloud as she threw a scornful stare at Harry.

Briefly, Harry stood rooted to the spot, for he had never seen a woman give birth, and also he was unsure how to handle the situation. Labour and delivery were never a part of the training curriculum at the military academy. The man was still lying at Harry's feet beseeching in a foreign tongue his innocence and mercy. Harry could see they were poor people and that it was too domestic and personal an environment for violence. He was suddenly disgusted and walked out into the sunlight leaving the man behind.

A few days later, Harry passed the huts and ran into the woman grinding flour as her children were sitting around, the older ones helping her with the chore. They threw him a hateful look. Through the interpreter, Harry was informed that she had had a miscarriage. Harry consoled himself that she already had enough kids and one less would do no harm in the long run. A novel abortion method for sure, he thought, smiling to himself: just barge into the delivery room, armed to the teeth dragging the husband behind. But for sure, these acts had contributed to the vicious cycle of militancy.

⊕

There had been intelligence inputs of renewed LTTE activity south of Puliyankulam and Harry was sent across to meet an EPRLF (Eelam People's Revolutionary Liberation Front) source for some information. Harry entered the room with the EPRLF man following. The source spoke a smattering of English and Hindi and claimed he had been trained by the Indians. When Harry had questioned him about India earlier, he had given an evasive answer. Harry wondered if he had picked up his Hindi by watching movies, because some of his sentences had a very familiar Bollywood ring to them. The source confirmed they had extracted whatever information they could from a suspected LTTE prisoner and the intelligence was actionable. There was LTTE movement on a disused jungle path that passed quite close to a Tiger camp in the jungles, east of Puliyankulam. Harry had insisted on meeting the source personally to corroborate the intelligence inputs.

It was a tiny dark room illuminated by a shaft of sunlight coming in through a narrow window on top. The floor seemed wet and slippery and there was a disagreeable dank smell. As his eyes got accustomed to the dark, Harry checked the walls expecting the prisoner to be sitting slumped in one of the corners and then he noticed him. The man or what was once a man, was hanging upside down from the ceiling, like a lump of meat one sees in a butcher's shop. There was just a slight sway as the body swung in and out of the shaft of light; the only indication that life still flickered in him. The EPRLF guy wearing a floral shirt and a lungi stood behind, a cigarette dangling insolently from his lips, as the smoke spiralled lazily up in the stillness. The sunbeam was bright, cutting across the room and one could see smoke and dust particles hanging in limbo. In the background somewhere, Harry could hear the loud buzzing of a fly—clearly disturbed by human presence, it was agitated now. The setting, Harry thought would be a film director's delight, for he had seen it often in movies. Except this was for real.

Harry felt no revulsion, for the man didn't seem human anymore. He was naked, with deep lacerations on his whole body. Clearly, whoever had interrogated him, wasn't too bothered about doing it scientifically and was only keen on inflicting pain. Like a drunk butcher being creative with a knife, he had slashed the body randomly all over. Blood flowed down those furrows copiously and that's when Harry realised the wetness on the floor and the odd smell were of fresh human blood. The body suddenly twisted and was face-to-face with him. All Harry could see were the whites of the man's eyes in the dark face, with the blood dripping off the lids, as they made contact with his eyes. He thought there was an appeal in those eyes or maybe he was imagining things.

'Shoot him,' said Harry sharply, turning away and shocked for the first time at this bloody apparition.

'Waste of a bullet *Saar*,' said Lungi the informer, 'he already dead.'

'No, he is not!' Harry insisted.

'Tell me *Saar* what do man feel most?' and Harry wondered where this was leading to.

'Let's see…umm…hunger, sleep…sex, oh,' Harry answered, 'ok I give up,' it was turning into a classroom charade with Lungi clearly pleased with his questioning.

'See, you react,' he said pinching Harry's forearm suddenly, 'it about pain *Saar*. Then see this,' and he stubbed the cigarette on the man's face. There was a slight sizzle of burning flesh and no reaction, not even the slightest flinch or muscle spasm. The man was clearly beyond pain. Point proven, he was dead, QED. Harry walked out into the sunlight an enlightened man. Welcome to Sri Lanka.

It struck Harry that the degeneration of a society could be gauged to a certain extent from the degree of violence it gets inured to and its changing mores on sex. The average Sri Lankan Tamil was way ahead in both these aspects. There was too much death and destruction around for them to get shocked any more and if life is uncertain and short, people tend to enjoy themselves while they can. Harry recalled someone telling him that in Vavuniya, *Lady Chatterley's Lover* ran to a full house for months, if not years. Only the Tigers and the IPKF were supposed to abstain from sex. But then, the IPKF had no choice and as for the former, they didn't need it, they had something better; they had the IPKF to fight against, for an adrenalin rush like no other.

That very night, Harry left for the post at Puliyankulam by road. By the time the rest of the team flew in the next morning with the team commander, Harry with his troop had already slipped out of the post, on a seventy-two-hour ambush operation. The going was initially easy, as they marched along a tar road, feeling rather exposed, under the bright light of what was called in the old American west, a 'Comanche moon'. Very soon the weight started telling and the men behind in the column gradually adapted the head down, shoulders hunched position, with the mind switched to drift mode, sustaining itself by latching on to more pleasurable thoughts of home and better times. Harry wondered what he would have been doing then if he had failed his probation and had been reverted to his parent infantry unit. He would probably have been attending one of the numerous boring parties in the mess in some peace station, or tucked in bed fast asleep. Then his mind drifted back to his probation in the Special Forces.

⊕

The first thing that had caught his eye as he walked into the Adjutant's office was a poster on the wall which said, 'People join us not because we are different, but because they are'. It was a standard army barrack with pictures and the usual assortment of trophies, and a large desk in the far corner. The Adjutant was missing, so Harry peeked out and the soldier on duty confirmed that the sahib was inside. Just when Harry was about to turn and leave, a thin voice from somewhere under the desk had asked who he might be. Harry saluted and rattled off his name and rank and that he was reporting for probation. A pair of eyes broke surface from behind the desk and sized him up. The face disappeared again.

'What are those elephants doing on your uniform?'

'Sir, I have been commissioned into the Madras Regiment. They are the regimental insignia.'

'Don't want any monkeys or elephants on the uniform while you are around here and take that bandmaster's dress off.'

Harry had found it unnerving speaking to a desk. Briefly, he wondered, if the Adjutant was playing with himself behind the desk. The weather was awfully cold; anything to stay warm. Half the face surfaced again.

'What would you like to do?'

'Sir, lunch would be fine.'

'Fuck your lunch!' the voice was quivering and in agitation the complete face was finally revealed. The Adjutant seemed to be shocked by Harry's answer. Harry figured out that there was a heater somewhere under the desk and the Captain had been warming his hands. He was clearly loath to be pulled away from it.

'I am talking about doing your PPT (Physical Performance Test) or BPET (Battle Physical Endurance Test).'

Harry had opted for the former, as it was an easier physical test—a mile run in PT rig (shorts and T-shirt) followed by a set of functional and flexibility exercises. He was told to report to the PT ground at 1600 hrs. With only thirty minutes to go, Harry just managed to dump his stuff and quickly change. His probation NCO Havildar Jai Baksh was waiting under a tree, hands tucked under his armpits, looking bored and disinterested. Harry noticed, he didn't wish him or stand at attention, nor did he ask Harry his name.

'What's your age sahib?' was his strange question, instead.

'Twenty-two.'

'Well, I am thirty-two and if you can keep pace with me, you will come in excellent timing.'

With that Jai Baksh had whipped around, clicked the stopwatch button and disappeared down the road at a fast clip. Harry had latched on to his heels like a bored dog chasing a vehicle, disturbed by his immodest remark and determined to make him eat his arrogant words. The road wound around the hill, past the MI (Medical Inspection) room and the officer's mess at a manageable gradient and Harry settled into his stride. He kept his eyes fixed on Jai Baksh's feet and maintained the distance, waiting for an opportune moment to overtake him. Then all of a sudden the road turned sharply and the gradient rose to a steep sixty degrees. Jai Baksh smoothly shifted gear, leaned into the slope and sprinted into the swirling mist at the top of the hill.

The sudden burst of speed stunned Harry and he lost all confidence seeing Jai Baksh's form disappear rapidly from sight. Harry couldn't believe anybody could run so fast. His lungs were complaining as he ran down the other side to see Jai Baksh, standing exactly the way he had met him; hands tucked under his armpits, not a drop of sweat on his brow, not a breath out of tune. To see him like this, when Harry was in a state of collapse, had shaken his faith in himself. If everybody was like this man here, Harry had thought, then it would be better heading back to the parent unit, instead of undergoing further misery.

'Fail sahib,' Jai Baksh had said.

'Can't be,' Harry gasped, bent over and clutching his stomach.

'In here,' Jai Baksh continued, 'if you don't make excellent timings you fail. There are no good and fair standards.'

'But those timings are for a flat course, clearly there must be some compensation for a mountain run,' Harry had retorted.

'Where is the mountain sahib?' Jai Baksh had exclaimed incredulously.

Soon, worse was to follow. The next morning was the dreaded BPET test. A two-mile run carrying a small pack, water bottle and a rifle in fourteen minutes and forty-five seconds. It was a test where even to fail one had to exert. There were thirty other soldiers present, a majority from the Madras Regiment and the rest from various other regiments of the army on their final leg of the probation. Each man a volunteer and eager to be badged into the SF. Amongst this rabble of nervous young men, with great equanimity stood a huge ram with an old jeep tyre around his neck. His name was Naal and he was the mascot of the unit.

Saved from the butcher's knife while the unit was on exercise in a desert somewhere in Rajasthan, Naal was attached to the MT (motor transport) section, on their ration strength and attended the PT parade regularly. However, age and senility were catching up rapidly with the old goat, noticeable in his erratic behaviour. He had been misbehaving regularly. Just that morning in a moment of mischief or ennui, one wouldn't know, as the senior JCO sat washing utensils in the tank, Naal couldn't resist the temptation to ram him in the butt and roll him over into the water. He was on a punishment run then and stoically bore it like an old soldier.

Harry noticed nobody seemed to regard the spectacle as bizarre. The Adjutant made a speech introducing him as a Madras Regiment officer and telling the men to ensure they stayed ahead of the sahib. Then he turned and reminded Harry, that as he was an officer and came from the same regiment as the men around who wore elephants on their uniform, he better lead the field. The whistle blew and the bunch took off, like little kids racing home after school. Harry saw the big ram weave his way through the crowd jostling for position, till he had galloped his way to the leaders. Naal was one hell of a competitive ram, Harry recalled with a wry smile—had he been a man he would have made a fine soldier for sure!

The entire bunch, along with the galloping goat, disappeared from sight around the first corner. By the time Harry sailed in, they had stopped taking the time, the men were into their second set of tests and Naal was chewing grass, having got rid of the tyre. This was getting to be humiliating. The Captain supervising the tests looked rather surprised, as if perplexed why a man couldn't run faster.

Anyway, the worst was yet to come—the dreaded speed marches—remembered Harry. 20, 30 and the 40-kilometre timed runs, lugging back-breaking weight. Harry remembered starting the 40-kilometre speed march, sometime at three o'clock in the afternoon, with Jai Baksh pacing him. With nearly 60 pounds, the distance had to be completed in well under six hours. The afternoon faded into evening, as the shadows lengthened across the road. Just over 30-kilometre and Harry had felt the first wave of fatigue sweep over him, his legs seemed like lead and he slowed to a walk. He recalled it was dark, when Jai Baksh shone a torch on his face to check for signs of dehydration.

All along he had been encouraging Harry to maintain the pace, but then strangely he suggested a stop. A villager on a bicycle had joined them for a chat and Jai Baksh very innocuously asked if Harry would like to place his pack on the bicycle. The villager agreed and offered to give Harry a lift too.

Briefly, Harry had been tempted, but his muddled mind told him there was something fishy in the offer. He declined.

It was standard practice, as he discovered later, when at a vulnerable moment in the speed march, the pacer would suggest shortcuts such as taking a lift. The slightest indication that an individual had succumbed to these offers meant it was RTU (Return to Unit) immediately. Harry vividly remembered the faint lantern lights in the darkness ahead, as he squeezed whatever little resolve he had left in him to make it to the finish point. The Adjutant had driven up from behind.

'You have seven minutes to spare. There is a bridge about half-a-kilometre ahead, you will touch it and be back. I will see you at the bridge. This is where we'll see if you are SF material or not.'

That was probably the toughest kilometre Harry had ever covered. In the SF they firmly believed in the adage that, 'It is not possible to know how much is just enough, until one has experienced how much is more than enough.'

The scouts stopped suddenly, jolting Harry out of his reverie. 'Snap out of the daydreaming,' he reproached himself, 'grief befalls you the moment you lose touch with the environment.' The lead scout pointed at a milestone which was a landmark and they veered right to enter the dark confines of the jungle. Another three hours and they arrived at a fire lane running straight like a ruler north. The men took positions and Harry settled down for the wait. On the third night, just when Harry had given up all hope of a contact, they heard the sound of a tractor approaching. The four kills they bagged, coming after months of toil, tasted sweet.

Bihar Company Post—Mannar

*If you take one step back,
You will never take another step forward.*
　　　　　　　　　—An American prison saying

From the road junction, Seven Troop was tasked to fly to the western coast and was attached to a Bihar Battalion in Mannar. For now, the exultation of the kills and Silvam's threats were quickly forgotten in the ceaseless and hectic pace of life and events. The usual jungle bashing commenced. Harry wished he had a book on the local flora and fauna, for at times he felt more like an armed forest ranger than a soldier. In the absence of any concrete intelligence, it was a gross waste of effort he thought, bushwhacking in the wilderness. With so much time spent outdoors, he wondered if joining the Indian Forest Service would have been a better idea. Harry loved wildlife as most of his childhood had been spent hunting with his father; however, after the last contact, the Tamil Tigers in the jungles had remained elusive like the mystical yeti. He wondered if Jim Corbett, with his tracking skills would have got better results tracking these Tigers. After all, he was once asked to track the notorious dacoit Sultana in the Terai belt.

The only difference there was the rations they carried. The Bihar mess they were attached to, packed fresh tiger prawns and Harry was a little taken aback when he pulled out his meal in the jungle. He ate the lot on the first day, fearing they may perish quickly in the heat. Later, when they came back to the post, he discovered the source of the prawns. The main road connecting Mannar to Colombo ran past the post and trucks loaded with the fresh catch of the day were stopped at the check-post for a search. As an unofficial toll, the driver offloaded enough fish to be allowed to proceed.

In the absence of any concrete human or electronic intelligence, the usual modus operandi was followed. A couple of prominent jungle and village tracks were identified for laying ambushes. Those were early days of electronic intelligence for the Indian Army and the crude direction-finders operated by the Signals detachment gave a general direction of any presence, suspected or otherwise, without a specific distance. Harry suspected their equipment picked up animal interference more often than human.

Since Special Forces do not hold ground, they depend on the local Company Commander wherever attached, for terrain and enemy information. No local commander willingly shared this information, especially regarding the latter, as it reflected poorly on the resident troops if the Special Forces guys managed to get a kill. Often the local commander intensified his operations when the Special Forces troop arrived, to ruffle the environment and ensure they didn't get any results. Intercepts confirmed that local LTTE cadres were also aware when a Special Forces team arrived and instructions were usually to cease movement and lie low till they moved on.

Harry heard the usual dreaded 'Jai Hind Sahib' and opened his eyes to see through his mosquito net a muted Sri Lankan starlit night and the silhouette of a palm frond flapping in the breeze, like the ears of an irritated elephant. Harry had been dreaming of home and for a second couldn't figure out where he was. There had been regular dreams of home lately. No doubt stress, privation and fear had a significant hand. Such had been the pace of movement that it took a while on waking to get his bearings right. The night before, Harry had got up to relieve himself and had walked into a wall hurting his nose.

The whisper became urgent as the man shook his arm. 'At two o'clock we march Sahib.' It took a bit longer this time for Harry to focus and he couldn't seem to explain the stars, the palm tree and the voice—familiar but unidentifiable. Harry thought he was still dreaming. All movement was done at night to maintain surprise and as the distances were short, on an average 10 to 15 kilometres, departure invariably happened post-midnight. The odd time made it difficult to get much sleep and the jungle in any case was too uncomfortable to get any rest.

There was a quiet hustle, as shadowy figures carried out last-minute preparations. Radio antennae were sticking out and Harry told the operators to twist them down. The men fell in and Harry walked down the rows, having a brief chat with the senior NCOs. He stopped suddenly, as the sharp smell of Lifebuoy soap jarred his nostrils in the clean night air. 'Alright, step out whoever has used the soap.' One of his men stepped forward.

'Mody, you know the orders, no artificial smells when we are hitting the jungles.'

'Just thought I will have a quick bath sahib,' replied the young soldier sheepishly, 'the next one will be after seventy-two hours. Have landed up with a rash in this muggy weather.'

'Well then stay back and enjoy your bath. You can't jeopardise everyone's life just because you can't handle a bit of rash. Show me the man who is not carrying some sort of a skin problem,' answered Harry angrily.

A final briefing followed, hushed prayers, cocking of weapons, the sound loud and incongruous with the quietude that otherwise prevailed. The team commander shook his hand, patted a few backs and wished them luck. The Biharis had lent two of their boys who knew the area around and they stepped forward to lead. The first few hours were across open cultivation and then the dark outline of the jungle was visible.

The initial part of the operation turned out to be a complete farce. First they lost their way and the Bihar boys spent an inordinate amount of time chatting and squabbling about direction. A track picked at random for an ambush was compromised as an elephant and her calf came calling. Harry could hear her trumpeting some distance away and got the men into an unused hut just in time as she got the whiff of human presence and went berserk, uprooting trees and bushes. Harry lay outside hearing her run amok in the undergrowth, with the rocket launcher cocked and ready, wondering if the anti-tank round would be good enough for a charging elephant and hoping he wouldn't have to use it. In the grainy green light of the night vision device, he could see her silhouette and the shining pinpricks of her eyes, as her little baby stood petrified, watching big mama throw a tantrum.

'Why is she so upset, what have we done?' whispered Girwar who was a desert man and more familiar with camels.

'Probably having her periods brother,' answered a quiet voice from behind in a Haryanvi accent.

Harry was relieved as the elephant's trumpeting faded into the distance. He peered into the darkness nervously and wondered what else the island was going to throw at them—a swarm of LTTE-trained vampire bats swooping out of the trees wouldn't be too out of place. But nobody wanted to step back into the jungle then and Harry decided to lay an ambush next to a village they had passed.

The next site was a thicket at the periphery of the jungle and turned out to be the crapping joint for the village next door. By first light, a dozen or so locals were sitting with them and beseeching Harry to be allowed to attend their call of nature. That's when he noticed the small pond behind them. Harry gave up and headed for home. It was a relief to be out of the jungle and be able to see the open sky. They passed the village school and some of the older kids had already arrived early to sweep and clean the classes. The other kids trotted along with the patrol, keeping their heads and eyes down.

The Sri Lankan Tamils took their education seriously. For Harry, one of the most endearing pictures in Sri Lanka was to see kids of all ages trudging off to school. Girls with oiled-pleated pony tails, a fresh flower tucked behind the ear, and the boys with a *tikka* on the forehead, always in clean white shirts, and come guns or guerrillas, bomb or bullets, the schools were never closed. As Harry watched the kids go by, he remembered a morning street scene in Puliyankulam. A few folks were buying vegetables, the usual pedestrians and a few kids of various sizes, with bags on their back, were heading to school. Suddenly there was a burst of fire from the sentry post at the corner of the street. The gunner was testing his weapon. However, the reaction on the street was predictable—everybody had hit the deck. The kids were the first to get up, dust their clothes and continued towards school; impressive commitment thought Harry.

That's why perhaps they were so good at improvised explosives. The education was put to good use. Harry wondered if their favourite subject was chemistry, or perhaps a specialised course called TNT or RDX or some such name. As they passed the village boundary, there was still scrub and undergrowth around, and in the distance he could see cultivation and huts. That's when he noticed slipper marks and a half-eaten biscuit packet tossed, it seemed, in a hurry, on a small path veering into the jungle. 'Well,' thought Harry, 'it's too early for a villager to be eating biscuits and heading towards the jungle.' He decided to investigate.

'Spread out,' he told the men, 'Sathish on point and careful, I have a gut feel there is going to be a contact.'

They carefully made their way back on the narrow trail through waist-high bush and were still some distance away from the jungle when Harry stopped to consult the Bihar boys for direction and read the map. That was when the team commander came on the line through their wireless handset. He was screaming something about an ambush, so Harry started to explain, when he was rudely told to shut up.

'You have walked into a bloody ambush Harry.'

As the words sank in, Harry's legs went weak and he cast a furtive look around, as if, any sudden movement might draw fire. The panic in the Major's voice scared Harry and he dropped the handset with the voice still screaming expletives out of it. His mind went numb and for some reason, he saw his mother's face and felt very very sorry for her. She never wanted him to join the army. Some of the men around noticed the change in his expression and as Harry sank first to his knees and then flat on the ground, the whole bunch followed immediately. Harry passed the word down, put them in a defensive perimeter and they lay doggo for the next half hour.

Silvam had spent the month recuperating from his gunshot wound in the Mannar camp. Being closest to the Indian coast, it was the best-stocked and often used as a transit base for the movement of LTTE cadres and their wounded to and from India. He was heading out of the camp when the sentry posted at the periphery of the jungle came running towards him. He was a young boy and clearly in a blue funk, as he blurted out the presence of the patrol coming on the path behind him. Silvam calmed him down and borrowing the sniper rifle from his buddy, shinnied up a tree. He had grown up climbing coconut trees and this big banyan was an easy climb. Through the telescopic sight he saw them half-a-kilometre away, coming in from the village end, weaving in and out through the scrub.

As he watched, his mind was working out the details of the opportunity ambush he would lay, for he had only four fighters and the kid clearly had yet to be tested under fire. Then again he knew the contact would invite reinforcements from the Indians and draw attention to the camp. His other concern was the young Indian woman journalist who he was supposed to escort to Mannar town and who was then following behind with the second party, at a distance. He got on the Sanyo walkie-talkie and spoke to the senior commander in the camp, a couple of kilometres further inside the jungle.

'Twenty-strong and well-spaced out Anna. It's the SF patrol which landed two days ago at the Bihar post. I am in position to attack.'

'How many will you get?' the commander asked.

'Should get the first three for sure, including the officer; the rest could manoeuvre around me.'

'Okay, break contact and link up with the party escorting the newspaper woman.'

The conversation was intercepted in real time by the Divisional Signals unit in Vavuniya and putting two and two together they narrowed it down to Harry's patrol out in the field. A quick call was patched in to the SF team commander at the post by the Colonel of the Signals Regiment.

Silvam watched them getting closer. He focused on a tall man walking third in the column. Clearly the officer, as the radio operator was just behind him. Through the telescopic sight he looked close enough to be touched. What a pity, Anna didn't want him to engage. If only circumstances had been different— the Indian woman wasn't along, the camp not a concern—he could have easily dropped a few of them. He studied the officer, who was heavily bearded, with his black head cloth loosely tied in a knot around his neck as a scarf. Nonchalantly he walked behind the two scouts, who were wearing body armour, and the group as a whole looked extremely alert. Something about the officer looked familiar, but he couldn't place it and before he could work it out, he saw the man stop and take the handset from the radio operator.

Silvam wiped the sweat off his eyes and a second later, when he looked again through the scope, the entire patrol had vanished. Desperately he scanned the foreground in a sweeping arc, back and forth, but there was no sign of them. Unbelievable, as if it was all a figment of his imagination. It just spooked Silvam, for he got a nasty feeling that perhaps they had got wind of his presence and may be stalking him.

Slithering down from the tree, he hurriedly retraced his steps back into the familiar depths of the jungle. Running into the group following him, he turned them around and hustled them back towards the smaller satellite camp.

Shradha Seth could see the panic on everyone's face as she was roughly seized by the arm and turned back towards the camp she had just left. She was amazed to see the man they called Silvam and who spoke passable English and excellent Hindi, in spite of his handicap, set off at a fast jog. There were other occasions in the last five days when army patrols had been sighted, but she had never noticed any sort of panic. The present situation was clearly different and in spite of not understanding all the alarmed jabbering in Tamil happening around her, the purport of the exchange was clear and for the first time since she had landed in Sri Lanka she was frightened.

She cursed her journalistic instincts and her desire to be a frontline conflict reporter. Why couldn't she have stuck to Bollywood tales like so many of her peers from the profession? It had taken her all of two months to fix the trip and it had involved meeting the LTTE contact person in London, who had dramatically, with a wave of his hands, pronounced how safe she was in the hands of the Tigers and that she would be given a chance not only to interview senior commanders, but also may participate in some live action if she was keen. And then here she was running for her life, like a guilty fugitive in an unknown jungle, from none other than her own countrymen!

After lying doggo for thirty minutes, Harry finally mustered the courage to order a move forward. Within a couple of hundred yards they ran into a tree under which they noticed footprints, boot marks and other evidence of a hasty evacuation by a body of men. He looked up the tree and knew instinctively where the sniper had perched himself and watched them and the thought of how close he had come to meeting his maker made his legs go weak and took all the fight out of him. In the previous camp the team had hit in the Muttur belt, his troop had taken a few IED casualties and had got stuck in a heavily-mined and booby-trapped area. They had been rendered useless thereafter for the rest of the fight and had to wait till the engineers could clear a path for them to come out. They had shared the nerve-wracking ordeal with him. It then occurred to him that if there was any experience worse than being stuck in the middle of a minefield, it was definitely the realisation that you were in the presence of a sniper. Harry turned to the senior NCO who had sidled up and was watching him intently.

'What do you say Zile?' he asked him in a whisper.

'Any further sahib,' answered Zile Singh, his brows knitted in concern, 'would be asking for trouble. For sure there is a camp in there,' he continued, pointing a finger into the jungle, 'and the only reason they didn't engage us, was to avoid a fight in proximity to the camp. If we go in unprepared like this,' and he looked at the body of men crouching behind and then gravely into Harry's eyes, 'take my word sahib, none of us is coming out alive. Call a gunship and take an approximate shoot.'

'Good advice Zile,' said Harry, 'suggest we spread out a bit in buddy pairs to receive any escaping parties that may come our way when the bombing starts.'

Harry hunkered down and spread the map on the ground and once he had worked out his own position, did a bit of guesswork on the location of the camp, narrowing it down to a couple of grid reference squares. There were all sorts of shoots in the army and this one, he thought with a wry grin, would be a lucky shoot. He called for air support and passed on the target grid references. Then he looked at his watch and waited.

Within half-an-hour he heard the distant drone of the approaching gunship. He signalled to his men to break up and get into their positions at the edge of the forest. Harry tried to peer through the jungle canopy to get a glimpse of the gunship, but his vision was limited. Then a resounding bang reverberated through the jungle, followed by the heavy clatter of the cannons.

⊕

Shradha was sitting with Silvam in a small satellite camp where they had stopped to get their breath back and where a few LTTE fighters could be seen gathering and preparing to take on the Indians. Silvam gave them instructions and then comforted Shradha who was looking noticeably scared. The information coming from the outlying sentries was encouraging. The patrol had halted and gone to ground.

'They won't dare to come any further,' Silvam confidently declared to her, 'an infantry patrol that came this way perhaps out of ignorance, but this bunch has learned from experience what happens when you try and hit one of our camps. In any case their numbers are not enough to cause us alarm. They are all dead men if they cross the big banyan tree.'

He had barely finished his sentence when the faint drone of the chopper was heard and immediately the whole camp exploded into a frenzy of activity. Radios came alive, tarpaulins were pulled across open mortar pits and everybody started rushing into the bunkers. Startled Shradha looked at Silvam who just uttered one word, '*Kotikai*' and then muttering the word 'crocodile' in English, he grabbed her by the wrist and ran out of the camp by another path. The group had barely gone 400 yards from the camp when the 500-kilogram high-explosive bomb hit the southern edge of the main camp. It was indeed a lucky drop, for the explosion obliterated and flattened everything in a radius of 20 metres. Trees crashed and mangled bodies flew through the air like rag dolls, some landing on the other side of the camp.

The damage would have been far greater had it not been for the thick trees which muffled the sound and impact by the time it reached the escaping group. Shradha was amazed to discover herself flat on the ground, for she had no recollection of having dropped to the jungle floor voluntarily. In a daze she saw herself being hauled up by Silvam and dragged down the path as the jungle canopy crackled to machine gun fire. Empty shell cases rained from above like hail, searing their way angrily through the foliage and hissing like angry snakes wherever they made contact with dry vegetation on the ground.

They made it to the periphery of the jungle with the sounds of death receding in the background. The group paused there, looking out over scrub country and the habitation beyond.

Silvam took stock of the situation and swinging east had barely gone a few steps when they came under fire. He had run into the last buddy pair deployed by Harry. Silvam detached two of his fighters to run the gauntlet of fire by drawing their attention, while he along with Shradha and two other men turned in the opposite direction.

Harry was standing in the open collecting the men, when he heard the helicopter gunship and looked up. As the bird turned, Harry could see the sinister bubble snout and the sun reflecting off its cockpit glass. He stood there looking at it and envying the pilots—no walking, no jungles and high enough to be safe. It was still circling innocuously like a vulture, but getting lower. It struck Harry that perhaps it was hunting for more game and like him, the pilot anticipated the prey to run out of the jungle after the bombing, offering an easy strafing target. Someone from behind in the column abused and remarked that it was going to attack. In fact there had been quite a few occasions of 'blue on blue' as the army called it, friendly fire on friendly troops, where gunships had been involved.

The Air Force had some of their choppers shot up early in the conflict trying to support ground troops and as a consequence the helicopter gunship made its entry to provide close air support. The only problem was that sometimes, they got too close in their enthusiasm to be able to differentiate between friend and foe. Among the few occasions the LTTE stations went on high alert and their radios crackled to alarmed chatter, was when the Indians used an 84 mm Carl Gustav rocket launcher, or the crude improvised automatic

SLR (Self-loading Rifle) called One Charlie, which had a tremendous noise and packed a nasty punch, or when a gunship was sighted prowling the skies overhead.

For a minute or so it disappeared from Harry's line of sight and when it reappeared it had dropped height significantly. Suddenly the heavy 'thock, thock' of the engine turned into the scream of a banshee and Harry looked up to see the MI-25, Akbar as the Indians called it, or the Crocodile, the name the LTTE preferred going by its looks, dip its nose and drop into a steep dive, like a hungry kingfisher scooping down on an unsuspecting fish. It was coming straight at them and Harry turned back to see some of the men at the end of the column disappearing into the safer confines of the jungle. Within seconds the trickle turned to a mini-stampede, as the lot scattered for cover. Harry shouted at them to stand their ground, for he didn't want the pilots to jump to any wrong conclusions. A couple of his men hung around with Harry, unsure on the course of action to be taken. He turned and saw the gunship bearing down like nemesis, the pilots visible at the controls.

He stood rooted to the spot mesmerised by the evil-looking iron bird of prey with the missile pods visible on its sides, as he expected one of them to explode to life with a flash any second. He imagined the pilot flicking the gun lever as they made a last bid attempt to verify the target with base operations before commencing the attack. The slightest hesitation on the part of the pilot, to use the 23 mm cannon or fire the 57 mm rockets… but the gunship did neither and instead opened up with a smaller machine gun, the rounds ploughing into the ground, thudding into tree trunks and randomly zipping through the foliage in a frenzy of destruction. Just 300 feet above them, it suddenly pulled up and roared away over the jungle. Perhaps the pilot realised he had been trigger-happy and had fired at his own troops, for the sound of the gunship receded in no time, as it flew back to its base in Vavuniya. Harry hadn't moved a muscle, as he slowly released his breath and looked back at his men, who were reluctantly popping out of the forest cover like ferrets, grinning sheepishly. Miraculously, only one man was slightly wounded by a splinter and he was quickly patched up.

As the troop headed out, someone noticed two people running in the shoulder-high bush beyond the effective range of their weapons. They reminded Harry of partridges being flushed out and he wondered if it was the Tiger ambush squad. He could see no weapons and hesitated but the scouts opened fire and Harry joined them gleefully in taking potshots. They then broke apart and ran in opposite directions and he saw their heads bobbing like rabbits amongst the thick undergrowth, till they disappeared from sight.

Silvam paused to look back when he heard the sound of the distant firing and knew his boys had managed to divert the attention of the patrol. Taking a detour, he swung back east and in an hour they hit the Colombo-Mannar main road. Hailing an empty truck on its way to Mannar, he put Shradha in the cabin with instructions to the driver to deposit her at the Bihar company post on its way.

'Remember,' he said turning to her, 'under normal circumstances we would have blindfolded you. Now you have a fair idea of the camp. However, you are a journalist and we trust your professional ethics. But,' he continued, massaging his wounded arm which had become quite painful, 'if people get killed on our side because of your loose tongue, then by God I will seek you out and slit your throat. They cannot interrogate you, so stick to the story that you hitched a ride from Colombo and were to meet a contact from our side who never showed up. And make sure you write nice things about us sister.'

Shradha was taken aback by the sudden threat, delivered by this mild-looking, handicapped militant leader and before she could respond, Silvam had slipped back into the shadows of the forest.

⊕

An hour later, shaken and tired, Harry hit the post. Another great outing came to an end in Sri Lanka and he worried if his poor heart could take much more of this adrenalin-pumping excitement. The Major looked at him expectantly to make some report.

'Nothing much to show Sir. A detailed after action report will follow, though I have a score to settle with a gunship pilot,' Harry replied.

'Perhaps you would have an answer to that,' the Major said, looking over Harry's shoulder.

Harry turned around and his eyes rested on the last thing he would have expected to see in an Indian Army post, in war-torn Sri Lanka; the figure of a fair young woman, slumped against the burnt-out trunk of a coconut tree, drinking tea. Handing his weapon to his buddy, he walked across and introduced himself. She looked shaken and utterly spent and even in her dishevelled state he found her to be pretty, in an intellectual sort of a way. As she got up and introduced herself, he realised she was tall and athletically built and her accent had just an insinuation of a foreign education. She rattled off the story already mentioned to the Major, about coming in from Colombo and not meeting her LTTE contact, but her words and condition were bereft of conviction.

Harry looked at her and smiled understandingly.

'You came out from there, Shradha,' he said, pointing towards the jungle, 'I respect your professional ethics and so will go along with your cock-and-bull story. But understand that in the final analysis, we are both batting for the same team and any information that helps in reducing Indian casualties, should justify breaching any code of conduct, or your so-called journalistic ethics.'

Shradha didn't contradict him, but looked away to hide her thoughts. Neither of them broached the subject again. She weighed him up quickly. Tall and gaunt, with humorous eyes. A shave, haircut and a bit of home-cooked food would do him good. She could guess he had just come out of the bush and in all probability was the man responsible for her sudden flight and her close shave with death. She could sense strength and violence, very delicately balanced in his quiet demeanour. As they talked, she discovered he had a dry sense of humour and a quick wit, which came from having soldiered, commanded and travelled. She realised that talking to him was the much-needed balm she required, to drive away her fear and fatigue and she also realised, that given adequate time, she would fall for him, head over heels.

As they chatted, intermittently her mind would drift to a different place, a different time and a very different sort of a man.

The man waiting for her back in the UK. Jagdeep was one of those well-educated, soft-spoken urban men. Physically he was shorter, but had the pumped-up body, that comes from working out in an air-conditioned gym. If he was balanced, predictable and boring at times, Harry on the other hand, seemed to be tottering on the verge of some unknown eccentricity, with an appetite for the unusual and the risky. If Jags was intelligent, this man was well-read. But the most noticeable difference was, that while Jags was an extrovert, Harry was an introvert, bordering on the loner. However, man to man, there was more depth in Harry than Jags had or would ever have. For that depth in character came only from life-changing experiences of having suffered loss, privation and solitude.

After a quick shower and a hot meal, Harry spent the rest of the day debriefing his men and writing his after action report. As the sun went down, Harry and Shradha sat out on camp chairs, enjoying rum and *pani* and listening to the sound of the cicadas rise in unison in the neighbouring jungle. That was the last cry of the wild, declaring the end of day.

The outpost where they were was a company post, strategically located, following a standard deployment format of saddling a main road. Towards the north and across the road, it looked out on open fields, some cultivated, others mostly lying fallow and running down to the sea further out. To the south and in the so-called backyard of the post, lay the thick wall of the impenetrable tropical jungle, separated by a mere 300 yards of clear field of fire. The trees had been felled and no undergrowth was allowed to grow in this belt. A prior negligence to ensure that the area be kept clear of any obstruction had cost the Sri Lankan army—who had manned the post before the

Indians—quite a few casualties. The LTTE, taking advantage of the cover provided by the unkempt undergrowth, had promptly crept up to the post at night and attacked.

The post itself was modest in size and accommodation. A few ramshackle, half-finished rooms provided living quarters for the two permanent officers in command and for any other SF units that arrived from time to time. A tin shed in one corner of the plot, meant for storing the local produce, along with tents pitched neatly in a row, provided lodging for the men. A shoulder-high fence, knitted out of palmyra fronds, separated the officers' quarters from the men's section and allowed for some much-needed privacy. For protection, a crude five-feet stone wall ran around the camp perimeter, reinforced with a roll of barbed wire fence, with empty condensed milk tins, filled with pebbles, strung along the complete length. Mines had been placed in the most vulnerable points of ingress and the four corners of the post had sangars (low fortifications of stone and sandbags), with machine guns covering the dead ground in front, in an interlocking arc of fire. The mortar pit was in the rear and the crew slept close by. The post was the only place in the conflict-ridden part of Sri Lanka where an Indian soldier could feel secure.

Harry glanced at Shradha furtively, finding her even more desirable, especially after she had washed off all the grime and dust of her jungle sojourn and with her short hair still wet. Having lost her rucksack which had a few changes of clothes—in the mad dash to escape—she had borrowed one of Harry's camouflage shirts.

'Don't go walking around in that shirt,' joked Harry, 'or you are liable to get shot. You and I have the same length of hair.'

As they talked about war, politics and travel, he discovered a woman cloistered in a world dictated by the dos and don'ts of society, dying to break free from its shackles. She was a soul yearning for some adventure and risk.

'You don't appreciate the full flavour of life until you risk losing it,' she said, quoting some wise philosopher who had clearly never faced death.

'I can see,' responded Harry smiling, 'your jungle experience hasn't given you the so-called flavour yet. Stick around some more and I guarantee, that quote won't be slipping off your tongue in a hurry.'

She was well-travelled, erudite and strong-willed, with views she wasn't prepared to change. For example, she was clear that the Indians were the aggressors in Sri Lanka. Dubious in their dealings, in wanting to run with the hare and hunt with the hounds, they had got themselves in a soup. And now the bully was getting whipped.

'Who says we are getting whipped,' responded Harry, feeling the need to defend the army, 'we are just hazy about the cause for this war. You know,' he continued, 'I hit a small camp the other day and guess what I found there! Bloody movie tickets of a theatre in India and a receipt from a private clinic back home. So we are all wondering, who's the bloody sucker in this play and are we being played around by our own side?'

Shradha was matching Harry drink for drink and they were half a bottle down, when Harry put the bottle away.

'We are both tired,' he told Shradha as she protested, 'any more drinking and we run the risk of passing out here. Not a good example to the men.'

'You know Harry,' she said, 'you nearly killed me in there. But no hard feelings, let me get back and I will develop a few pictures I took of the camp and militants, if it is of any use to you. But I did get the feeling and I may be wrong, that the Tigers are just whiling away time till the IPKF leaves and then they can get back to sorting out a smaller Sri Lankan force.'

It was around midnight and rather late by Sri Lankan socialising standards. Harry got up to escort her back to the independent room which had been vacated by two officers, so that she could get some privacy.

'I have a hectic day in office tomorrow,' Harry said in jocularity, 'and in here, there is a saying, "The only easy day in office was yesterday."'

They walked back to the room holding hands, as if it was the most natural thing to do. In silence they stood briefly, immersed in their thoughts and neither ready to part. Then they kissed, a long lingering easy smooch. Things could have progressed further if the footsteps of the sentry hadn't sounded. The guard duty was changing and they came apart quickly. The post, while safe, was also the last place where a man and a woman could get any kind of privacy for intimacy.

Next morning, there was the usual activity at the post that preceded the arrival of a chopper. A protection party went out on a patrol to sanitise the area, while a detail of soldiers stood at standby for unloading the rations. Another bunch stood around chatting happily with their colleagues. You could make out from their body language and expressions, which were the ones heading homeward on a spot of leave. Generally everyone was excited about receiving much-awaited letters and the fresh food that came with such sorties. Even with an untrained eye, Shradha could easily make out the difference between the infantry soldiers on the post and the SF men. The latter with their beards and long hair, looked lean and fit and had an indefinable aura of those who had seen hard combat and that too, a lot of it.

They were aloof and clannish, hanging around in buddy pairs or their allocated squads and even in the safe confines of the post, each man carried his personal weapon. For in the SF, one's rifle and ammo come second to none. You can fight without water and food, but you can't do without your weapon, went the adage. Every man was reminded on joining the unit that he would spend more time with his rifle, while he served, than with his wife. Over time the weapon became an extension of the body and a man felt naked without it.

Shradha finished a hurried breakfast as the chopper came in to land, raising a mini-dust storm. The tin roof on the shed clattered in defiance and the palm fronds bowed in the mighty downwash. With so many people around and the din created by the bird, Harry barely managed to whisper a word or two, before the Major practically pushed her into the chopper. In exactly ten minutes, the fresh supplies and ammo had been unloaded, the leave party had settled in and the chopper was airborne again in a cloud of dust. For the men left behind on the ground—their excitement abated in the time it took for all the dust to settle down. By the time the flying machine was a speck in the sky and its sound a mere buzz in the distance, the post was already back to business as usual—a fighting patrol to be sent out, live goats that had come in as fresh rations to be slaughtered, ammo to be distributed and a bunch of other activities, which go into keeping a post fighting fit.

India and Back

The price of anything is the amount of life you exchange for it.
—Henry David Thoreau, *Walden*

With Shradha out of the way, Silvam's thoughts turned to the crisis in the camp. By the time he returned, a semblance of order had been restored. They had four killed and ten wounded, out of which Anna the camp commander was the most serious case. One side of his face was disfigured, with the skin hanging like a peeled banana and his body, as if it had turned into a powerful magnet, had attracted shrapnel of all sizes and shapes, riddling it into a gory mess. But he was still alive and his bloodshot pleading eyes met Silvam's as he stood looking down at his old commander. Silvam turned his gaze away wondering how a man could still be alive in that wrecked state. Why couldn't he just peacefully die and cease that pitiable moaning which was demoralising the others. If it had been on the battlefield, Silvam was sure he would have begged Anna's forgiveness and shot him.

The LTTE senior command reacted quickly and arrangements had been made for an immediate evacuation of the wounded that very night by speedboats to India. Men would be waiting to receive them at Rameshwaram, from where the casualties would be taken by road to the town of Tiruchirappalli (Tiruchi). Silvam was ordered to lead the team and then stay back in Madras to escort a VIP Indian politician to Sri Lanka. He was to wait till further instructions and lie low at an LTTE sympathiser's house.

Under the light of a waning moon, the two speedboats slipped out into the dark grey sea. Barely 3 kilometres out, they sighted an Indian naval vessel—a frigate about 500 yards to the starboard and moving silently like a ghost ship, its silhouette etched clearly in the muted moonlight. The speedboats cut their engines and waited. Low in the water, they were a difficult target to be picked up by radar or by the night watch on the Indian ship. Silvam wondered how the boat's pilot had sensed the presence of the ship, for he could barely see the other boat 50 metres ahead. However, these were no ordinary fishermen, but trained members of the LTTE's nascent naval arm. Each man carried a cyanide capsule, like the other fighting cadres of the LTTE, hung on a chain and worn around his neck like a signature locket. It was the LTTE's deadly equivalent of a name tag worn by regular soldiers going into combat. The capsule could be used with fatal consequences, should the need arise. LTTE cadres were trained not to surrender but to choose suicide by biting on the cyanide capsule instead, if their capture was imminent.

Suddenly the ship was sighted turning around and the pilots of the boats swung into immediate action. There was no panic or alarm in their movements, as they gunned the engines to life and swung the boats away. It struck Silvam that perhaps the ship was making a normal manoeuvre and their sudden flight would certainly give away their presence. The last thing he wanted was to die in a high sea chase, without even having put up a fight. He had no idea if they were heading towards the Indian coast or going back to Sri Lanka, for in the excitement of the moment he had completely lost track of direction. But the boatmen knew from experience and instinct and needed no compass or fancy positioning systems for direction.

By the time the frigate completed its turn and got into the chase, the speedboats were lengthening the distance between them. Then the sea was lit up like a day, as a star shell burst overhead, shredding bare the safety provided by the cover of the night. Silvam felt naked, as if his clothes had been stripped in a public place and he ducked instinctively. The speedboats started to weave a crazy pattern at maniacal speed, as the first of the machine gun rounds started to stitch the water around them. A shell exploded close by, buffeting the boat and drenching everybody to the skin. Silvam braced himself for the end and prayed it would come by a shell or a bullet, rather than by drowning or in a worst-case scenario, by cyanide, if captured.

At some stage during the chase, the speedboats parted company with each other and sped off in opposite directions to confuse the frigate. With their heads ducked below the gunwale, none of the passengers noticed they were not together or that the boats had outstripped the ship and managed to lose the hunters in the vast expanse of the ocean. Silvam raised his head to look around when he felt the boat had stopped and the engine was idling. He saw the Indian ship in the far distance, desperately firing star shells in an empty sea, as a spotlight from the deck futilely scanned the water below. Silvam was wondering what had happened to the other speedboat, when he saw its shape glide out of the darkness and come alongside. His admiration for the LTTE crew went up by several notches. Blind navigation, extreme manoeuvres, brilliant seamanship and link up. This was as professional as one could get.

That's why the naval cordon had been ineffective. With such seamen, which cordon wouldn't be? But Silvam wasn't to know that the senior commander wore no cyanide capsule around his neck, but instead carried Indian identity papers confirming him as a fisherman from a village close to Tiruchi in India. He was as Indian as they come and a professional smuggler to boot. He had no interest in a Tamil Eelam or the IPKF for that matter and was slave to none, bar money. His services were being paid for. The crew exchanged a word, comforted the passengers and then set course again for the Indian coast.

They landed on an isolated obscure spot of the coastline and were met by the local LTTE support team. Out of the six casualties they had carried, four were dead, including the popular camp commander Anna. Silvam was glad to get his feet back on firm ground and collapsed on the sandy beach in a heap. The overdose of adrenalin pumped in his body during the thirty-minute chase, left him exhausted and utterly spent, like a woman after childbirth. They buried the four men in a clump of coconut trees and covered the area with bush. Silvam silently mourned Anna's passing—a fine man and a close friend. He did not know the other three men.

The local group quickly took charge and the injured men were whisked away to a private clinic, while Silvam was taken to Rameshwaram and left at the LTTE safe house, run by a sympathiser. Strangely, Silvam felt safer in India, then he had ever felt in his country, inundated as it was, with trigger-happy soldiers constantly seeking to harm him. He stepped out of the house in the evening and was reminded of Jaffna in more peaceful happier days. But what he ached for, was a visit to the mountains. It was a strange dichotomy in his temperament, which allowed him to love all things Indian in India and—with an equal measure of hatred—destroy all things Indian in Sri Lanka.

Through his source he found out about his next assignment and was told, no movement of the Indian politician would happen for a month or so, as Prabhakaran wasn't sure where he would be and also the risks were too high. With a month to kill, Silvam—on an impulse—decided to head north on a nostalgic trip. The cold season had set in and the weather would be perfect, for he loved the bracing winter of North India. Tying up with the local contact that he would make an STD call every alternate day to stay in touch, he bought himself a second-class rail ticket to Delhi. Like a child, he found himself a window seat and sat glued to it throughout most of the journey. This time there were no restrictions and the freedom was intoxicating, especially when he reminded himself that he was heading into the heart of enemy country.

As the train crossed into central India and entered the Hindi-speaking belt, Silvam got the opportunity to practise the language he had lost touch with and by the time he alighted at Delhi station, he had got his tongue around most of the words he had forgotten. The multitude of people, the constant chaos, his familiarity with the language and the overwhelming size of the country erased all fear and apprehension he had carried about being caught. With a new-found confidence, he strode out of the station and took an inter-state bus to Dehradun. The sky remained overcast most of the way and the weather got colder as he proceeded upcountry. In Muzaffarnagar, he got off and bought himself a monkey cap, jacket and a cheap camera—for he wanted to capture the trip for his wife. He reminded himself to pick up a toy or two for his young son, a very affectionate kid. Every time Silvam left home, it broke his heart to part from the boy and his heart-wrenching weeping, and the picture of him clutching his mother in misery would stay a long time with him. The two of them he realised were his only weakness and he desperately wished he could somehow get them out of this mess. With Prabhakaran also having taken a wife, the rules around matrimony had been slackened by the supreme commander and one didn't necessarily have to hide his marital status.

In Dehradun he went around to all the shops he used to visit when he would come down for the weekly shopping trip, during his course at Chakrata. Some of the shopkeepers recognised him and enquired where he had been. He took a local Vikram, a public autorickshaw and got off at the Forest Research Institute building, for he had always passed it on his numerous trips to the city and admired the scale of the structure. Posing in front of the imposing facade with the mountains in the backdrop, Silvam asked a passerby to take his snap. From there he strolled across to Vasant Vihar, the residential colony just across the road.

With some difficulty, he found the way to his old instructor's house, for he had always come in a covered bus and had never really managed to have a good look at the route. A lot of new houses had sprung up in the colony and the trees had grown larger. The bougainvilleas were in full bloom. The previous day's rain had washed the mountains clean and they were shining fresh and green, with the tin-roofed houses in Mussoorie shimmering in the crisp sunlight. It was a beautiful day and a far cry from the death and violence of Sri Lanka.

Silvam stood under the arbour of some silver oak trees, across from the Colonel's house, deep in thought. Now that he was here, a decision taken in haste, he wasn't sure if meeting his old instructor was such a good idea. They were after all at war and none other than his son was serving in the army. The Colonel knew all this and might not be as friendly. He could easily inform the authorities and if caught, the intelligence he carried on him would be disastrous. It would be a bloody stupid way to go down, trying to pay respects to your old guru and getting hauled up in the bargain. The door opened and he saw the Colonel come out with his dogs. He hadn't changed a bit in retirement. Silvam wished the circumstances had been different, for he would have loved to talk about the operations and the war. Briefly, the Colonel glanced in the direction of Silvam, who promptly pulled his monkey cap further down and looked away. The dogs rushed out, eager for a run, the Colonel followed and stood under the porch, affectionately gazing at his dogs frolicking in the winter sun. Then leaving them at play, he turned and went in and the door closed behind him with a bang.

Silvam stood there inhaling the crisp cold air and feeling alone in a foreign city. In that instant he felt the load of his responsibility—the chosen path of his life as a freedom fighter—bear down on him, with the weight of the mountains in front. What was he doing here? Taking unnecessary risks, when every man counted in the fight. He should be back home, leading his men and not enjoying a personal holiday. Suddenly, the whole place seemed too peaceful for his liking. It was all unreal, a chimera in a world to which he didn't belong. And for the first time in his life, the realisation dawned on him, that the old accountant was dead, to be replaced by this seasoned dog of war and that he would never be a man of peace again. The LTTE had not only taken away his real name, but also his temperament. Shiva the man of peace, had turned into Silvam the man of war and strangely, he wasn't mourning the loss of the former. Turning, he retraced his steps to the bus station. Within forty-eight hours, he was back in Rameshwaram at the LTTE safe house.

Three days later, he got his orders to link up with another detachment of LTTE operators. The politician's trip had finally come through and the op was a go. He was waiting with five heavily-armed men at a deserted strip off the Tamil Nadu coastline, when the Indian politician joined them. The flotilla of four speedboats, with armed cadres sailed out. They stopped briefly to rendezvous in mid-sea with an Indian fishing vessel to refuel. The vessel was supplied by the local fishermen who got a quota of 1,000 litres of diesel per boat at a huge subsidy from the Indian government. Selling part of that fuel at three times the cost was more lucrative than fishing.

'Strange war,' thought Silvam, as the boat was getting refuelled. The fuel, food, training, weapons—everything to sustain the war effort came from the Indians; in fact the LTTE's safest bases were in the country of their enemy and their casualties treated in India, and on top of that, the Indians threw in four divisions for the killing, as a cherry to the icing on the cake. At this rate, he mused, once they had Eelam in Lanka, carving out the state of Tamil Nadu to join them wouldn't be too difficult. With tanks brimming with the much-needed gas, they sped onwards, towards one of the many islands that lay off the coast of Jaffna.

Jaffna

The only thing I know is that I know nothing and I am not quite sure that I know that.

—An old agnostic

After months of jungle bashing, Seven Troop got a breather and was ordered to move to the suburbs of Jaffna for an area domination role. They broke journey in Vavuniya briefly, till the Air Force could arrange the airlift. With nothing to do, Harry took the men out for a run around the airfield perimeter. There was a bit of grumbling, but it was good to build up a sweat and the feeling of openness and safety was a refreshing change for everyone. Months of jungle bashing had sapped all the stamina and even as a distance runner, Harry felt the heaviness in his legs. The sun was setting over the palm trees, as they ran past a couple of gunships, with the technicians working on them. It reminded Harry he had a debt to clear with a gunship pilot. The faint sound of drums and cymbals from the local army temple wafted across the field. The evening *arti* was in progress and God was much in demand across the island. He heard one of his men Anil's sonorous voice leading the singing session.

A Sri Lankan Bell helicopter came prancing across the tarmac, barely 50 feet over the ground and the gunner gave Harry a friendly salute. In the evening Harry strolled across to the pilots' mess. All quarters were in tents, strung in a row along the airstrip and the officers' mess occupied the largest canvas. There were a couple of pilots lounging around still in their flying overalls. He was welcomed immediately with a drink. Harry inquired about the op discreetly and it took the Squadron Leader, who was the senior-most officer, some time before he figured out which sortie Harry was talking about.

'Oh! That is Bharat you are talking about, the Mannar shoot. Don't tell me you are the guy who asked for it.'

'Well, where is he then?' replied Harry, 'I have come a long way to thank him for taking a shot at us.'

There was an awkward silence, as the pilots sensed the menace in his voice. The Squadron Leader stepped in to clarify.

'Bharat's on leave. But let me answer on his behalf, as we had a good chat about it later. Firstly, you weren't in your given location and had moved a considerable distance. Then you were seen emerging from the jungle and on sighting the gunship, some of the men made for cover. And let's face it Harry, you guys didn't exactly look like regular soldiers, with beards and flowing hair. Look at you for example, if I saw you in my gun sight, emerging out of a forest full of bandits, I wouldn't think twice about pulling the trigger.'

'Touché,' retorted Harry.

'Because Bharat was unsure,' continued the Squadron Leader, 'he didn't fire the rockets, instead he fired a warning burst or two from his machine gun. I am told one of your men was nicked, well bad luck. Let me tell you partner, you wouldn't be standing here if he wanted you dead. Now have a drink.'

The next day two MI-8 choppers carted them across to the Palaly airfield from where they made their way to Kokkuvil, a suburb of Jaffna. There had been a sudden spurt in LTTE radio traffic and the military top brass suspected either a big strike or the movement of some senior LTTE leader. The troop had to quickly adapt and change their drills to the urban role, which after months of jungle ops was not easy. Harry realised that contacts in built-up areas would be sudden, sharp and short and so he ordered rifle slings to be removed. All patrolling was to be done with the weapon at port and ready to engage. If the close confines of brick and mortar, streets and alleys were a bit of a nightmare for patrolling, the abandonment of the heavy packs they had lugged was a reason for joy. But it was good to be back in civilisation and for some R&R a video cassette player and a television set were arranged on rent and movie cassettes procured from the Jaffna market.

The three vehicles, which had carted them across from Palaly airfield were held back by Harry and gave him some mobility. He decided to expand his beat area, and in the bargain, do some tourism and sightseeing. The first was a trip to Jaffna University, the site of a disastrous operation by one of the sister Special Force battalions. There was also a desire to relive his college days and interact with some of the students. Harry was aware of the Jaffna University operation, which had taken place before he had landed on the island. In a way, the real beginning of Operation Pawan was the assault on the university headquarters of the LTTE. The plan was to make a lightning raid to kill or capture some of the top leadership, including Prabhakaran. The plan had gone horribly awry.

In a swirl of dust, the vehicles stopped. Harry could see and feel the tension amongst the students and the restrain not to panic. The slightest indication of violence from him could have led to a stampede. The attempt to maintain a facade of normalcy was noticeable, but it was a veneer, and one could observe hurried steps and furtive nervous glances. Harry walked into a class and regretted it immediately. The chatter died to a frightened hush as dozens of young eyes were fixed on him. The teacher withdrew into a corner and Harry felt extremely conscious under the scrutiny of so many eyes. Most of them would have been a couple of years younger than him. There were quite a few girls and suddenly Harry was aware of his unkempt beard, faded-torn dungarees and all the accoutrements of war. It was a place of learning and peace and deserved respect. The loud clomp of military boots echoed a jarring note to the sensibilities. The gallant and dashing Lochinvar image faded a little and Harry handed over his weapon and ammo vest and told the men to wait outside.

It took a while for them to open up but once they knew Harry meant no harm, the opinions rolled thick, fast and unanimous. The Indians must leave. Harry focused on a dark, sharp-featured, pretty girl with shining white teeth and plaited-oiled hair. She was bold in her gaze and questioning, and he admired her courage. They spoke in broken English and Tamil, and there was a clamour, as all of them wanted to have a say at the same time. So Harry asked them to raise hands, and took the questions. It was like a college town hall with headmaster Harry, taking it upon his young shoulders to defend the country and army in an open debate. Needless to say, the pretty girl got more chances to vent her feelings.

'*Saar* what if we come, take your house,' went one of her questions, and Harry nodded gravely, with a frown of resigned repentance. The longer Harry stayed, the prettier she looked, and his one-sided interest was obvious to some of the boys, who smirked and nudged each other. While no one openly displayed pro-LTTE sympathies, it was clear, they all wanted peace, and if there was to be any sort of subjugation of the population, then it rather be by the Tigers than by the Indian Army. There was no gratitude and the Indians were solely blamed for becoming the problem rather than the solution. Harry walked out disappointed. What a gross waste of good Indian lives and to what purpose!

The only heartening sight was the girl with the white teeth and a taste for North Indian men. Harry recalled the lovely dark face as the vehicles pulled out of the campus, the quest for life in those young eyes, as they flirted just so slightly, smiling broadly and raising her hand enthusiastically all the time. It struck Harry that most of the houses he had visited while patrolling for a search or just for a glass of water, had mostly only women family members. They wouldn't speak much but their sad eyes would follow you everywhere. The men, he was often told, were either working abroad, dead or had disappeared, which meant, in all probability they had joined the LTTE. What a waste of good womanhood, thought Harry pensively.

It was early morning and still dark and in the absence of any street lights, the silhouette of houses and palm trees stood out starkly against the fading starlight. Harry was on an area domination patrol and survival was about denying the enemy the opportunity to hurt you. They set no pattern to their movement, timing and route. The patrol drifted around aimlessly, cutting barbed wire fences, jumping over boundary walls and switching lanes often, with a general sense of direction to be taken and the time they need to be out. This kind of patrolling, other than putting the wind up the LTTE, because of a complete unpredictability of the movement, also gave very little chance for the Tigers to lay an opportunity ambush. Harry knew because the radio intercepts confirmed the LTTE's dilemma and concern.

Harry saw a faint light in one of the houses and decided to investigate. Ten minutes of knocking and there was still no response. All the loud knocking and kicking of the door was creating quite a din. Anywhere else the ruckus would have passed off as a domestic row, here it could only mean one thing—an IPKF patrol had come calling. Harry was worried about drawing fire. Their presence was known and all it would take was an insomniac Tiger to pull out his weapon from the well and let off a few bursts, then get back to bed before his wife even noticed his disappearance.

He surrounded the house and broke in the door. In the dim yellow light stood a young couple clutching each other for confidence and courage. Harry took in the scene quickly and weighed them up. They were genuine and safe and he allowed himself to relax. Harry noticed the woman then and she took his breath away. In fact there was a mass sucking in of breath, as the four men with him, inhaled all the air in the room simultaneously and then there was pin-drop silence. Nobody moved, nobody exhaled, it was like playing statue and the only movement was of her bosom heaving at a frightful pace. Harry thought a bosom was designed to convey extreme distress, other than its normal functions; well this one was for sure.

Harry noticed she was light of colour in comparison to her race, with sharp features, wearing a purple nightgown, which fell shy of her knees and barely managed to cover her bosom. Her right breast was threatening to pop out now in her agitation and Harry observed it had a large black mole halfway down that broke cover every time she inhaled, which was quite often in her existing state. He was fascinated by the mole, as were the others in the room. It looked like a huge tick and Harry had this urge to pull it off. She reminded him of someone he had seen in a porn flick. He got the impression perhaps the couple were in the middle of a session when they had intervened. Imagination was kicking in and Harry saw Anil Pehlwan lick his lips, horny as the town bull. The couple was mumbling their innocence in good English and Harry heard something about both being teachers at the Jaffna University, as he wrenched his attention away from the black beauty still playing peek-a-boo with the audience.

The loud gunshot report stunned everyone; it stopped Harry's heart briefly for sure. Mentally he felt for pain in his body and then cast a quick glance around, expecting one of his men to slither down. Thoughts were racing through his mind and then he noticed dust at his feet. The EPRLF boy who was with his troop as a guide, in his nervousness or excitement (probably the latter) had accidentally blown his big toe off. There was a pool of thick dark blood collecting around his bathroom slipper and his big toe lay neatly severed, a couple of inches away. Strangely, it reminded Harry of a lizard's severed tail and he expected the toe to start wriggling away any moment.

Before the EPRLF boy could register the loss or pain, his weapon was snatched away and attention focused on him, as everybody pitched into him verbally and physically. It struck Harry that had the shot hit 6 inches to the right, it would have been his toe wriggling away. He would have earned himself the wound medal for sure, shot not by enemy fire, but by a sexually aroused boy, barely out of his teens. Harry was so shaken, that he thanked the boy for sparing him by punching him repeatedly in the face.

A furtive look by Harry confirmed the heaving bosom had picked up pace and was probably matching her heartbeat now. With all this vigorous movement, the gown seemed to be fighting a losing battle and was on the verge of slipping off. It was a situation Harry was not confident of handling and for sure he thought, if she didn't get herself under control soon, they all ran the risk of shooting themselves in various parts of their anatomy. He stepped in to chat up the couple and pacify her lest she became hysterical. Her name was Latha and Harry called her husband *thambi* (younger brother).

Once they got over their fears and realised the soldiers meant no harm and the officer was rather friendly, Latha divulged some information. Two streets away, she had recently noticed a couple of LTTE fighters at a tea stall. It was one of those pieces of unsubstantiated loose intelligence, uttered in times of duress, to please the security forces in any protracted insurgency area. Harry didn't take the information seriously, but decided to swing by as the distance was not too much.

As a parting shot, Latha very innocuously warned Harry to place a guard when the men go out for their morning call of nature. Apparently the Tigers had noticed a pattern and were keeping the latrines under surveillance.

The sun was up as they parted company from the couple. Harry decided on a long circuit to approach the street, before winding up for the day. They entered the street and he told the boys to spread out. It was a typical Jaffna suburban residential lane, with small independent houses on either side separated by palm frond fences and the ubiquitous palm and banana tree in each plot; very little to differentiate it from a street anywhere in Madras. The houses were neat, but in need of repair, and the overall impression was of a place which had seen better days in a forgotten past. Under the shade of a huge jackfruit tree, a small shop selling the usual daily needs saddled the street midway, where a group of people were milling around chatting, drinking tea and buying the odd victuals for the day. A half-naked little boy went past wheeling a tyre with a stick. The tyre had a close resemblance to an Indian Army Jonga tyre. Harry wondered where he had got it. Probably his papa had given it to him as a souvenir after blowing up a few good men....

A dog and a bitch were joined, coupling away and quite oblivious to the gathering crowd, while another dog watched silently with its tongue hanging out in envious lust, hoping for a chance. It was copulation day in Sri Lanka it seemed and Harry smiled wryly at the thought. The aroma of spices was sharp and pungent as breakfast was being prepared in many homes. It smelled much like dosas and the thought of food erased Latha from his mind. Suddenly there was commotion in the crowd and then four men get onto cycles and furiously pedalled away in the opposite direction. Now, no one in his senses ran away from an IPKF patrol unless they were guilty. So Harry shouted for the men to stop and then to the assembly to lie down or disperse, so as to get a clear line of fire. But this bunch stayed put, in fact he observed they were closing ranks and the intention in those few seconds was quite obvious—they were helping their brethren.

There was a hollow bark of an AK on semi-auto mode as Sathish opened up. Harry took note; it was the second time Sathish had fired on suspicion, for no weapons were visible on the men. He was not sure where the bullets went, probably knocked a few coconuts, but the result on the mating dogs was unprecedented and instantaneous. They violently uncoupled and Harry saw the dog turn and run past through the patrol and down the lane. Sensible dog, though the same could not be said for the locals. Not one man, woman or child had even ducked; they sure were a seasoned lot; Special Forces material to a nail. The next instant, the four musketeers had turned the corner and the last guy let off a burst over his shoulder, perhaps in mock salute, Harry wondered, looking at their poor marksmanship. It was pointless giving chase, as they had a head start, were on cycles, and were familiar with the area. A well-aimed burst from a rooftop or a blind corner and he would be buying casualties for sure. Then a young man broke away from the gathering and made a break down the street. Instantly Sathish gave chase.

The youngster couldn't have committed a bigger folly, for he was trying to outrun a handpicked man, who had been trained to cover 40 kilometres carrying 60 pounds of unwieldy weight in under six hours and then be fit enough to fight.

His flight to freedom was doomed from the moment it took off. The soldiers and the locals watched the outcome of the contest with bated breath. The youngster suddenly veered right in an attempt to shake off Sathish, who was fast closing the distance, and tried vaulting over a waist-high fence. His foot caught the edge and he toppled over. Sathish sailed over the fence, like a hurdler, landing lightly on the other side, with the young man sprawled on his stomach at his feet. A gasp of anguish went up from the gathering. Harry couldn't help applauding the ease and panache with which Sathish had reeled him in. He was reminded of lines from Chekhov, 'When a man spends the least possible movement over some definite action, that is grace.'

However, he was furious. Months of toil and they had lost the only chance of getting a kill because of that lot. He lined up all males above the age of fifteen and the only confirmation he wanted was that the youngster and the four who got away were LTTE cadres; a simple affirmation of a fact. But it was *'illae* Sir' (no Sir) to a man, down the line. Tempers were high, their adrenalin was pumping and so they resorted to some basic street questioning methods, which were quick, unimaginative and ineffective from a results point of view, but highly satisfying to quell one's bloodlust. It was lots of boot, butts (rifle and human) and the rest of the anatomy no-holds-barred. Harry recalled, it was called a 'Chicago Stamping' in one of the James Bond books that he had read and this one lasted for ten minutes.

They rolled back to the post, which was a semi-independent bungalow in Kokkuvil. Everybody was feeling better after a dose of violence and permission was sought to issue rum.

As most IPKF posts were attacked by the LTTE at night, all drinking as per local army orders was to be done during the daytime—a sure way to turn one into an alcoholic. A few more years of deployment in Sri Lanka and Harry was certain, cirrhosis of the liver would end up claiming more IPKF lives than the Tigers. Sufficiently inebriated, they got to work on the young man they had caught, who they found out was called Shankaran. In the late 1930s, Sir Charles Tegart, who had policed Calcutta 'very efficiently' for thirty years, was brought in to police Jerusalem. He introduced what was called the 'water can' method, whereby water was forced down a prisoner's nose using coffee pots. The Americans call the practice 'waterboarding'. The Indian Special Forces in Sri Lanka, however, had their own name for this interrogation method—*tanni* (water) parade. The methods might have differed, however, principles of all three remained the same—to give one a taste of drowning.

There are various nuances to the practice and a master practitioner can actually drown a man for a few seconds, before bringing him around. Harry was not sure if technically death was due to asphyxiation or drowning, however the difference between death and life was precariously balanced on a few seconds of breath either way. A few seconds more under water and you could lose the man, while a few seconds less and a determined man could play along for hours. Harry recalled an Urdu couplet quoted quite often which was appropriate to that scenario, which went:

There are only two states in life.
This state—the living—and that—the dead.
Between the two states, the distance is of just one breath.
While it runs, it is this state and when it stops; it is the other.

The pros whom Harry had studied under, would often take a deep breath along with the victim and time the duck accordingly. A hardened case, Harry had seen once, lasted seven such duckings before he cracked. In sheer admiration his interrogators had served him an omelette. Then there were occasions when water was not so freely available for a ducking and a cloth was stuffed into the mouth. Water was then poured down the cloth, while clipping the person's nose. The latter was a slower process and more frightening than the former, as the interrogator had less of an idea about how much water had been poured into the prisoner. So Harry was told by an enlightened soul, who had undergone both forms of interrogation. Harry had wondered if the guy ever went under a shower thereafter.

The man Shankaran however, was not made of such mettle and the moment his head was pulled out of the bucket, he started to sing like a canary on cannabis. The atmosphere changed immediately and Shankaran was offered or rather forced to have a drink. Never having touched alcohol in his life, the potent Indian rum hit him like a six to the fence, for he got up, staggered a few steps and then crashed awkwardly on to the table, made out of ammunition boxes.

'Hey, you will damage our expensive table,' retorted Sathish.

Everybody had a good laugh, including Shankaran who dissolved into an uncontrollable giggling fit, like an adolescent virgin. It was prime time entertainment for men who had found very little to laugh at in months. By the time he was three pegs down, he was positively cursing the LTTE for ruining the country and was prepared to sell their mothers to the nearest bidder.

'The local Tiger squad *Saar*, was escorting a senior commander, when you people turned up. But more important, is a small camp in the Alampil jungles,' he said, his speech heavily slurred, 'I delivered a mobile Honda genset there some months ago. This one is a screen defence and the camp around 8 to 10 kilometres further inside, is one of the biggest. I can take you in till the first one though.'

But Alampil was way beyond their area of ops and Harry showed no interest. An interrogation report was sent to the Divisional Intelligence Officer and Shankaran was packed off to the nearest brigade headquarters. The Intelligence Major read Harry's report, had a brief chat with Shankaran and packed him off promptly on the next convoy to the Gurkha Battalion at Kumulamunai, responsible for the Alampil area. The news about a camp in the jungles there was stale, for everybody knew it existed somewhere in that piece of green real estate. The question had always been, who would walk into the Tigers' den?

Harry visited the lane of their last patrol after a couple of days, to be greeted by sullen looks. The damage was noticeable with swollen faces and broken limbs among the local residents, but they seemed to have got back to life with a vengeance, including the bitch, busy coupling with a different dog. But everybody it seemed was back to normal, barring the few aches and pains.

⊕

Unbeknownst to Harry, Silvam was ensconced in a house just behind the tea shop. He had landed back from India, escorting the AIADMK (All India Anna Dravida Munnetra Kazhagam) politician. Having seen the boat crew in action on his way to India, Silvam had sat confidently through the journey back.

He knew with experience that their speedboats were much faster than anything the Indians could throw at them and the guys knew the waters better. In any case, Lady Luck was on their side and the crossing was uneventful, except for bearing with the politician, who was constantly throwing up throughout the trip like a drunken sow and soiling the entire boat.

They made their landing on one of the small islands that lay off the coast of Jaffna. From there along with a band of twenty fighters, Silvam made his way to Kankesanthurai at the northern tip of the island. There, the politician was handed over to the next man in the chain responsible for conducting him further, with the final destination known only to a few. 'Clearly,' thought Silvam, 'he was on his way to meet Prabhakaran, to be running such risks.' A message came through that Silvam had been promoted to the rank of a Colonel while he was away and he was ordered to head down south, to take command of the unit in the Alampil area.

Breaking journey at Kokkuvil, where he had lived years ago while working in Jaffna, he stayed the night at his old landlord's house, who welcomed him with warmth. There was never a fear of anyone informing the army, as the entire population to the last man, was pro-LTTE. The local Tiger squad was supposed to drop him off at a bus stop, from where he would go by road till Kilinochchi. If you weren't carrying a weapon the possibility of getting caught by the Indians, at the many check posts they had strung across the island, was nigh to nil. He was having his morning cup of tea and chatting up the locals, when suddenly round the corner, the Indian Army patrol materialised most unexpectedly. There was no question of getting into a firefight with so many civilians around.

Time slowed down, as if to fill the space between them, giving him adequate opportunity to notice that the men wore black bandanas and beards. He knew instantly where he had last seen them—in a jungle, through the high-powered telescopic sight of his sniper rifle. Unbelievable, same unit, a second time and for a fraction of a second, he thought he recognised one of the men in the column as his old instructor's son, but before he could confirm his suspicion, all hell broke loose. The next instant he was sitting behind on the carrier of a bicycle, with the Tiger boy peddling furiously and his two accomplices covering the retreat. There was the thump of gunfire from behind, one of the fighters fired over his shoulder in reply and then they took a turn to disappear in the warren of narrow alleyways that dissected the town into a chaotic maze.

Silvam heaved a sigh of relief; the gods were on his side, for no mortal can cheat death so many times. While killing had become business, of an enemy who had remained largely faceless, discovering Harry's presence bothered him. For the first time there was a face to the enemy, whose father had been his guru and whose hospitality he had partaken of in a foreign land. But the coincidence was unbelievable. He didn't want to be the instrument of Harry's death. After all that was the least he owed his old guru.

Getting off at Kilinochchi, Silvam made his way to Kumulamunai where he spent some time with his wife and young boy. He was told a new Gurkha Battalion had replaced the Sikhs in the location and in the evening he took his son out for a cycle ride on the road, which went past the post on the hillock. Silhouetted against the darkening sky, a few figures could be seen on the hill, the only sign that human life now existed on that piece of high ground. For no villager had ever occupied it. Even the stray dogs and cattle avoided the high ground and children were forbidden to venture up the hill for the locals believed, the place was evil, with a potential to heap great misfortune on any mortal desecrating it by inhabiting the ground. The villagers had subsequently built a temple at the base of the hill, to appease and contain the malevolent evil spirits.

The Indians of course were ignorant about the local superstition, not that they would have changed the location if someone had mentioned it to them. For the hillock, by any standards of defensive deployment, was the most strategic ground to hold and perfect for dominating the area around. Silvam however, was aware that a hundred-plus foreign souls, dangerously-armed, were ensconced in an area half the size of a football field, with intent to do him and his brethren harm. That was his area of operation and the unit freshly inducted. Moreover, he neither believed, nor had the patience to wait till the evil of the place unleashed its calamity on them. It was a capital target, plain and simple and waiting to be punished. It would also establish his leadership in his new command. He made a mental note of that.

The village was also the entry point to one of the biggest camps the LTTE had in the Alampil jungles next door. One of his tasks therefore, was to ensure the Indians didn't stray into LTTE country, for with the urban centres under heavy IPKF control, if the LTTE were to get expelled from their jungle hideouts, it would be nothing short of catastrophic—the end of the game. The only way Silvam knew to dominate an area was to take the fight to the enemy. He waited and prayed for the opportunity and the opportunity didn't take long in coming. The moment the tents and the radio antennas were up and the bandobast necessary for the conduct of war was met with, the camp vibrated with energy akin to a live beehive. Patrols could be seen going out in various directions for area familiarisation, choppers replenished rations and warlike stores, and the local headman and seniors from the village were summoned for a quick powwow with the Colonel. In a very quick time, there was an air of purpose and action amongst the troops.

Silvam was in a small hamlet, dealing with a suspected informer, when news came of a large column of Gurkha troops reportedly streaming out of their post and heading towards the jungle hideout. Silvam was immediately summoned by none other than Mathaya, the second in command in the LTTE hierarchy after Prabhakaran, who was in camp then and personally briefed him to stop the advance.

'Mark my words Silvam,' and Mathaya's gaze was steady, long enough to emphasise the importance of his order, 'you must first try and discourage them from proceeding any further, for I don't want any attention coming this way, while we have an important guest from India. But if they resist, annihilate them to a man. The severity of the punishment must be an example to deter them from ever straying into the jungles, for the rest of their stay here.'

Gurkha Battalion HQ Post, Nayaru Lagoon

When first under fire and you are wishful to duck,
Don't look nor take heed at the man that is struck,
Be thankful that you are living and trust to your luck
And march to your front like a soldier.

—Rudyard Kipling

The Commanding Officer (CO) of the Gurkhas was a tall strapping man who had practically grown up in the unit from the time he was commissioned. The Colonel was what they called a regimental soldier and nowhere was it reflected better than in the affection he got from his men, which he reciprocated in equal measure. To command your own unit was every soldier's dream and to do so in war was the apogee in his profession. He was sure of his standing, a confident leader and certain the men would follow him to hell. With his senior Company Commander, he stood now at a vantage point, next to the machine gun nest, surveying his area of jurisdiction spread below, with the trained eye of a soldier. The Colonel inhaled sharply, smelling the salty sea air which was heavily laced with the smell of fish, enjoying the peace, the maintenance of which, he knew, would decide his career.

To the west, the sun was an orange blob dissolving into the glimmering lagoon and turning it red. The village of Kumulamunai was behind him and hidden by a grove of dense coconut trees. A smaller hill, 600 yards to the left, interspersed the patchwork of otherwise flat open fields. In between the two hills, a small area had been levelled to provide a makeshift helipad. A narrow dirt track hugged the coastline and ran past the two hills to disappear into a copse of wild coconut and banyan trees in the distance. A lone cyclist with a small child could be seen on the track, adding a certain tranquility and normalcy to the scene. An open field stretched in front for half a mile, giving a clear field of fire, beyond which could be seen the dark green line of the jungle. In a few minutes another day would come to an end in Sri Lanka. The Colonel looked wistfully towards the distant jungle and turned to the Major.

'That's where the beast is,' he said, with a nod of his head, 'and that's where we should seek him. Two months and I haven't heard a shot fired in anger. We will have to stir ourselves Shukla, or perish of boredom. Is the LTTE *podiyan* (a low-grade messenger or courier), what's his name—Shankar something, the guy passed on to us by the Jaffna brigade, is he ready to lead us to the satellite camp?'

'Doesn't seem too keen to venture out of the post Sir,' answered Major Shukla. 'Shit-scared. He knows his way only till the smaller camp, but apparently the mother camp further inside is huge. Says, if you go in, you will stay in, none will come out. He's overestimating the calibre of his old pals or underestimating our fighting prowess. Anyway, will get the boys ready and the moment the leave party rejoins in a few weeks, we hit the road.'

A couple of weeks later, a company strength-plus, self-contained for forty-eight hours and led by none other than the CO personally, set out on a seek and destroy mission. Shankaran made a determined attempt to dissuade them for the last time, pointing out their unpreparedness, but his pleas were brushed aside and the column boldly marched out in broad daylight. If only the CO had read Mao, perhaps he may have understood what the prisoner was desperately trying to convey—that in waking a Tiger always use a long stick.

But then, except for artillery shelling, there are few things in the field of battle that can easily deter a hundred-plus quality fighting men. Especially, when they belong to a regiment whose battle honours cover the world and run the length of your arm. Bravery was a byword with these men, encapsulated in the motto, that 'it is better to die, then to live the life of a coward.' Paeans had been written about their courage and the first Field Marshal of independent India, Sam Manekshaw, himself a Gurkha officer, had once remarked that, 'Anyone saying he was not scared was either a liar or a Gurkha.' Such men then, had little to fear.

As they approached the jungle, they were fired upon and the men went to ground. The fire was desultory and from a distance. The CO consulted the forward platoon and ordered them to continue with the advance as the firing was ineffective. Spread out, the column was nearly half-a-kilometre long, as it wound its way through secondary jungle like a languorous giant snake. Shankaran at this stage made another feeble attempt to drive some sense in the commanders, but the die was cast and the heavily-laden men marched on till they reached a thin strip of land, with the jungle on one side and the sea on the other. If a piece of real estate was ever designed for an ambush, that little plot would have scored a perfect ten. Even under more peaceful circumstances, the most accomplished practitioners of the art of ambush put at the receiving end would have found it nigh to impossible, if asked to extricate themselves under fire. The only counter was, what the training manuals often teach in such a situation—to turn and assault. And yet even that was not possible, for the distance from the firing point to the killing ground was neither too close for an assault, as most would have been cut down in the intervening space and nor was it too distant for the fire to be inaccurate. And whatever few deficiencies were thrown up by the terrain, were quickly made up by the ingenuity of the LTTE commander in the use of ground. This then was where the bulk of the column was engaged and stopped by a large body of hostiles. The column splintered and in the absence of any coherent command and control, the situation turned rapidly into a fight for survival and then degenerated into a rout.

⊕

Silvam, having selected his ambush site, a narrow wedge of land saddled between the lagoon and the jungle, waited with a bunch of fifty fighters. A couple of Tigers kept a watch on the column from the time it moved out of the post, keeping abreast of their advance and rolling back gently all the while, as it advanced. When the party was halfway to the jungle, Silvam ordered his men, via the radio, to fire some warning shots.

'Make sure there are no casualties,' he warned, 'or we will have them baying for blood. Just enough to dissuade and turn them about.'

He heard the gunshots and waited anxiously. Shortly afterwards his walkie-talkie crackled to life and he heard the breathless excited voice of the squad leader.

'The column is on the move again Sir. Should I drop a few to stop the advance?'

'*Parva illae*, don't worry Kumaran. Fall back gradually and lead them to the point. The reception party is waiting.' Deep down he was pleased they had persisted in continuing, for he could now follow Mathaya's orders and teach the Indians a lesson that they would not forget for years to come.

From the edge of the forest, Silvam watched the patrol trudge past barely 30 metres away. Timing it to perfection, he waited till the column was midway down the thin strip of land before giving the order to engage. A hundred yards of the jungle suddenly erupted into a hail of devastating fire. There was pandemonium amongst the ranks, as the soldiers ran helter-skelter to save themselves. But there was no place to hide and the only cover available, which was the jungle, was where all the fire was coming from. The CO, with his party along with the vanguard platoon, was trapped and pinned down. The proximity, volume and the accuracy of fire was such that the column was viciously torn asunder in the middle and all control lost, as platoon and section commanders tried to get a grip on the rapidly deteriorating situation. With a slackening in command and in the absence of any coherent orders, the tail end of the column promptly turned around, seeing men from the leading sections fleeing back. A running fight then ensued over a couple of kilometres, with the contact becoming individualistic, as groups fought their way back. Finding no way out of the killing field, some of the soldiers jumped into the lagoon.

A body of men, with the CO and the Subedar Major (SM), however settled down to what would be the last fight of their lives. The savage trading of lead continued through the night, with fire from the small group of Indians gradually dwindling by the minute. Sometime during the night, the Colonel, who had been wounded early in the fight, closed his eyes forever to the world. The morning brought no cheer to the remnants, as they expectantly looked around for some succour in the form of reinforcements. Grossly outgunned and running short on ammunition, the last few Gurkhas did what they had done best for centuries. Pulling out their kukris, they charged the enemy as a body and were promptly cut down within seconds.

Like a member in a participatory Greek theatre, the stout, handicapped Colonel of the LTTE watched with grim satisfaction as the macabre dance of death was played out. The result of the ambush was better than he had anticipated and he exhorted his men over the din of battle to make each shot count. Silvam didn't have to give any orders to cease fire, for it finally stopped when there were no more targets to be shot at. He waited for a few pregnant minutes and then gingerly stepped out to inspect the carnage. The ground was littered with bodies and gear and to the gently murmuring sound of the waves in the background was added the forlorn moaning of the dying and injured.

The Tigers then walked amongst the fallen, taking head shots to put the wounded soldiers out of their misery. Silvam knew there would be retaliation and the place would be swarming with troops shortly. With no half measures in his dictionary, the job was still undone. He was going to follow the second part of Mathaya's order to the letter and set such an example, as to render the unit unfit for combat. With a wry smile, he then recalled the words of his instructor in Chakrata.

'When you have your man down,' the old Colonel had said, 'don't hesitate to kick him hard between his legs, till he bawls "papa".'

Professional soldiers are predictable, thought Silvam, and more so if they have been your trainers. He was well acquainted with their standard operating procedures. Having mauled the unit, he knew retaliation was imminent and a troop build-up would follow as a precursor. The nearest landing zone was the Gurkha post and that was where he would head. If the plan formulating in his mind went well, he would crown the success with a chopper to his name. Splitting the team in half, he led the raiding force back to the village of Kumulamunai, using tracks and paths unknown to the IPKF.

From a distance he could see frenzied activity in progress on the post. The news of the debacle was filtering in and the disquiet it had created was visible. Silvam went straight to his house and warned his wife to pack up and take refuge in the stone temple next to the sea and away from the mayhem that he was about to unleash.

'Wait for me, for I will join you for sure, and look after the little boy,' he told her, as she stood there petrified, clutching her son to her bosom, with a profound sense of foreboding gnawing at her innards. 'Don't venture towards the village for the Indian dogs will be rabid by then and will bite anything Sri Lankan—man, woman or child. Wait for a few days and in case you don't hear from me, then assume I am dead.

Keep this address, go across and meet this man. He will help you. Stay out of this madness for I see no end in sight. Give the boy a peaceful environment to grow up in, an opportunity destiny has denied us.' Pulling something out of his front pocket, Silvam slipped a folded piece of paper across to her.

The villagers were then told to assemble in the local school and those showing reluctance, such as the old and the sick, were herded by force and a guard posted to ensure no one would contact the IPKF post. Silvam knew from experience that the first reaction of the soldiers would be to take their anger out on the nearest village, which by their expectations, should have warned them about the impending attack. With the locals taken care of, Silvam along with fifteen men parked himself on a high ground, 600 metres away from the post, with the helipad below and in his direct line of sight. There he waited, like a patient hungry vulture.

Post-Road Junction

As for man his days are as grass; as a flower of the field, so he flourisheth / for the wind passeth over it, and it is gone.
—Psalms 103:15-16

The sojourn at Kokkuvil came to an end and Seven Troop was asked to move back for jungle ops. Harry looked despondently for the last time at the little bungalow, the bustling street and the shops which had been home for a few weeks. The basic comforts of civilisation like electricity and toilets were addictive after having lived rough for months, and with a heavy heart, the troop boarded the chopper for Kilinochchi.

Harry had lost count of the number of times he had moved locations. In his opinion, it was all a waste, with no return on the efforts put in. This time it was a Kumaon company post they were attached to and the moment the *langar* (cook house) was functional to churn out puris, it was rock and roll in the bushes. It was supposed to be another of those never-ending ambushes and Harry was just settling down for a long haul when he got a message to abort and head back to base. He was getting a feeling that these outings were designed more to keep them busy rather than kill any Tamil Tigers.

He now feared dying of prolonged boredom in the bush, more than by enemy fire. Harry was temperamentally not designed to sit immobile for so long and often got the urge to run out screaming, or throw caution to the wind and just be normal for a change, a sort of picnic in the bush. 'It was only from the point of view of stillness that one understood motion,' he reminded himself for the umpteenth time. 'You are a renunciate, a pilgrim, Harry Baba, this will only make you stronger. Stay the course, everything passes, perishes and palls.'

He had heard of road rage and wondered if the symptoms he displayed at that point could be classified as bush rage. Maybe, he mused, a new kind of ailment had been discovered by him; depression due to sustained exposure to the bush, culminating in insanity, wherein the patient finally starts thinking he is the bush. He comforted himself by recalling the words of FS Chapman—a man who had spent three years in the jungles of Malaya during World War II—'There is no good or bad jungle, only the mind makes it so; the jungle is neutral.' All talk in the jungle was in whispers or sign language and even back at base it was not strange to find people still continuing conversations in whispers.

By the time Harry got back to the post, the Major had already departed with the rest of the team. The operator told him it was an SOS op and a big bird was coming in to pick them up in twenty minutes. Packing took no time as they lived off their backpacks and moved every week or so. In jocularity they called themselves the whores of the army—anyone could take them.

The MOH (meat on hooves, in army parlance live goats) had been delivered and the men herded the four goats to the helipad. The MI-8 circled over the post and lost height rapidly in what seemed like vertical drops and settled down in a cloud of dust, engine whining and rotors running. It was the helicopter version of the Khe Sanh style of landing and take-off. Harry recalled reading it was during the siege of Khe Sanh, an American base in Vietnam, where the pilots perfected the art of landing fixed-wing aircraft under fire. Basically, just short of the runway, the pilot did a vertical climb and then corkscrewed straight down, before pulling out just in time to land. The Russians followed the same trick during their stint in Afghanistan to avoid the Stingers and rockets. The pilot signalled to Harry to load and pointed to his watch. Landing and taking off in Sri Lanka was when those guys earned their flying allowance.

A few choppers had been knocked down or damaged by the LTTE and the pilots were very jittery on the ground. In fact the unit had lost an officer while attempting a jungle insertion. The chopper was on a low hover over a jungle clearing and the officer was standing at the door managing the winch, when suddenly they received heavy ground fire. The pilot pulled out immediately and the chopper limped home damaged, carrying the officer dead. A single bullet had slipped from under his bulletproof vest and met his unfortunate heart. Clearly, it was preordained, for how could one explain that the very clearing in the vast jungles selected randomly from the map had the Tamil Tigers taking a coffee break, when they saw this gift from heaven descending and emptied their magazines at it in joy.

The pilot then revved up the engine to indicate his impatience and the bird hopped a little. The men were crammed like rounds in a magazine, with their pots, pans, plastic sheets and bamboo poles, along with the goats. It looked more like a bus full of slum dwellers being rehabilitated than a military chopper carrying SF troops. The chopper lifted a little, struggled half-heartedly and settled down in a cloud of dust. The Sergeant chatted into the radio set briefly, leaned across and told Harry to reduce weight. Out went some bamboo poles and a sack or two of flour, but the Sergeant was insistent on ridding them of the goats. An argument ensued and the co-pilot joined in the discussion.

Tempers were rising and in spite of the shouting, most of the conversation was getting lost in the din of the engine. 'One man's meat is another man's burden in this case,' thought Harry. 'Unbelievable, such a big chopper and they were haggling over a couple of hundred kilograms!' He was briefly tempted to put a pistol to the pilot's head to force him to take off, like one sees in the movies where the hero threatens a doctor or a pilot to save his men; of course, in this case, it was goats! However, something told him to keep his own counsel. The Air Force would have been bloody pissed if they had lost one of their choppers for a couple of goats. Needless to say, Harry would have lost his neck for certain. It was hard-earned proteins for sure and in an environment where food occupied a huge part of their thoughts. After all, what else was there for a man to fight over? The three Zs—*Zan, Zar, Zameen*—women, gold and land, as the Afghans say are worth fighting and dying for, and all were missing in that case.

The bird had been on the ground for over fifteen minutes and the crew was getting noticeably nervous now. A sitting chopper drew the Tigers like pirates to pillage. They just couldn't resist the temptation and would have a go at it with whatever was available—small arms, rocket-propelled grenades or mortars. Three goats were put down reluctantly and they were still overweight and then there was muffled report of automatic fire somewhere and immediately the whine of the engine picked up. There was rattling on the fuselage, as if someone was showering pebbles on it and people exchanged worried looks. A soldier pointed at the roof and Harry shouted at the Air Force Sergeant to either let them out or take off. The chopper shuddered violently in protest like a drunken dragonfly, hung in brief uncertainty a few feet over the ground and then, to the bleating of goats and clanking of pots and pans, it lifted off with a jerk.

Harry wondered if the Kumaonis providing helipad protection had lost patience and fired a few shots, enough they knew to end the argument and give the pilot the boost he needed. After all one would rather lose men than a chopper on your real estate, it was not good for the post commander's dossier. The pilot circled over the post, gaining height, till he was out of range of small arms fire, before putting the nose down and heading out. It was only when they were airborne that Harry realised he had no idea where they were going.

The chopper flew further south and looking down the open cargo hatch, kaleidoscopic images flashed past; from dense green jungle to a mosaic of open cultivated fields criss-crossed with dusty tracks and roads. They crossed a broad tar road, the A-9, the main artery connecting Jaffna in the north to Colombo further south. At the junction of some of these crossings, thatched cottages popped up and finally they could see a stretch of scrubby, sandy white beach. The chopper turned over the green-blue sea and approached an open area, dotted for miles around with coconut trees. They were on the north-eastern coast next to Nayaru Lagoon and the place was called Kumulamunai.

From the men standing around, Harry knew it was a Gurkha Battalion post. They directed him to a hillock about 400 metres ahead, on which he could see tents, radio antennae and other indication of army inhabitation. The moment he mounted the hillock, he got the strange sensation that something was seriously amiss. A body completely bemired was lying in a foetal position next to the track. He was a local and showed no sign of life. There was listlessness about the men in the post and most carried a vacant stare, as if in deep shock. They were hanging around in groups like people are wont to do after an incident. There was an unnatural hush about the place and the feeling of death and loss was all pervasive.

Harry ran into his Commanding Officer who had landed earlier with the CO of a sister SF unit. The Colonel was talking quietly to the 2IC (second in command) and the Adjutant of the Gurkha unit, telling them something about this being a war. Animated chatter in Gurkhali came from inside the communication tent, as a soldier came out and reported that another party of five had reached the post at Chemmalai. A little later, Harry heard Hindi songs being played in the tent and the same soldier came out looking helpless and dejected, to report that all radio channels were jammed by the Tigers and they were playing, of all songs, '*Sare Jahan Se Achha*'. Harry got to know the story from the team commander.

Forty-five men were missing, with a few having turned up at

another post. The CO and the Subedar Major were missing and believed killed. It was a standard practice the LTTE followed—of mauling a fresh unit so viciously so as to render it incapable of any further aggression during the rest of their stay. A little later, the Division Commander flew in and gave a pep talk to all the officers and JCOs. It was a war he told them and people died, or words to that effect. Next to arrive was the Brigade Commander and he had the misfortune of commanding the hottest brigade in Sri Lanka. There hadn't been a dull moment since he had deployed the brigade and the Brigadier was looking for a quiet evening to write a few letters home, when the news of the debacle was reported. As night flying was not allowed he commandeered the Div Commander's returning chopper the next morning to make his way to the post. He was a Guards Officer, nattily dressed with a red scarf and a product of the best training institutions the army could provide. A briefing had been arranged for him behind the mess tent.

It was around nine in the morning and already the armpits were running like a tap. A large map hung in front and chairs had been arranged facing it, in neat rows. Even in a calamity situation the army's bandobast was not forgotten. People took their seats. The two COs along with the team commander and the Gurkha officers sat in front. Harry sat behind with the commander's chopper pilots. A Major stood to brief them with the help of a map hung on one side of the mess tent. He was the officer commanding or was commanding, what was left of the ill-fated company, which was still accounting its dead and missing. Bedraggled and tired, he looked traumatised. The Brigadier opened the briefing in a very refined accent and said something about being 'here not to criticise but to learn from our faults'.

The Major narrated the sequence of events and talked about how they were caught in the open with no cover and how the intensity of the firing broke the column into two. People insistently enquired if he had seen the Commanding Officer and why was the body left behind. Leaving the body of a dead comrade behind is humiliating, unacceptable and a shameful act and if the bodies happened to be those of your CO and SM, the crime was unpardonable. The Major claimed, the last he saw of the CO, he was severely wounded and the SM was along with him. Apparently, the SM refused to leave his side, stating that he preferred to die, rather than desert the man he had practically grown up with. Whatever the folly of the plan, clearly courage in some quarters was not found wanting.

A volley of questions were directed at the Major and Harry felt rather sorry for him, as he was completely outranked and got no chance to get a word in edgeways. Everybody was seething with anger and waiting for the Commander to lay out his plans for retribution. His further inquisition was interrupted by a burst of gunfire.

The Brigadier arched a questioning eyebrow.

'Tell the post sentries to stop firing. I said no noise while the briefing was on. They are probably engaging the fishing boats out in the lagoon. Continue Major.'

Before the Major could continue, the firing escalated and there was a dull thud of a mortar bomb. Someone came running to say the post was under attack. The Brigadier was ushered into the dug-up mess tent, while his pilots raced downhill to the bird parked below. Within minutes they got the chopper airborne and Harry watched amazed, as it flew backwards barely 20 feet above the ground, away from the firing. There was panic on the post, as every man with a weapon blazed away at some unseen enemy. Harry looked around for his senior JCO to get the troop ready. Some of the men were having a bath at the well and turned up in an assortment of clothing. Six Troop was told to take a detour via the village and approach the high ground from where the fire was coming. They disappeared down the hill at a jog, while Harry with his men went down towards the helipad, taking cover behind a boundary wall that ran around a temple. The team commander joined him there.

The firing had intensified and Harry was unsure what to do next, as he crouched safely behind the wall. A glance over his shoulder and he saw a ragtag bunch of men. There was Sathish, his shirt open to the waist, a gold locket around his neck and a huge grin spreading across his black face, with eyes practically oozing wickedness. He sure loved a good fight. Anil was in shorts and singlet carrying the heavy rocket launcher, his brow creased in anxiety and big droplets of sweat pouring down his face. Zile Singh, all 6 feet of him, looked like a harried Humphrey Bogart, with tousled hair and furrows across the forehead. He was in a pair of red bathroom slippers with a bandage around the left foot. Harry peered around the wall and decided that the only way to dominate the firefight was to make a frontal assault.

The combat logjam demanded sheer aggression, but Harry couldn't seem to get his limbs to move. It was raining lead. He stayed put, shouting something behind at the men. The inability to move bruised his ego, for it went against his temperament to be cowed down like this and he berated himself. The fear of being thought a coward gave him courage and he stepped out from behind the wall. There was a rattle of musketry from very close and Harry stopped, crouched and watched the pebbles do a tango a few inches in front of him, as his fear-addled brain tried to make sense of that phenomenon. Then it hit him, he was the target and it prompted him to do an ignominious back roll, to retract quickly behind the safety of the wall. He heard the Major shouting something about getting the men killed. His mind was going numb with all the orders and noise and Sathish didn't help by prodding him with the barrel from behind and whispering in his ears to take the lead.

There was a militant sitting on a tree across the compound and Harry indicated this to the Major. Someone then emptied his automatic into the foliage. Harry recalled a saying by Robert Clive, 'To stop is dangerous, to recede ruin'. He took the plunge and ran down, pausing for breath at the bottom, to get a better picture of the contact. 500 yards away Harry saw five or six figures wearing lungis and camouflage shirts, under a knoll, quite oblivious to all the fire being directed at them. He ordered Anil Pehlwan to fire the 84 mm Carl Gustav rocket launcher for an airburst and the shot was a beauty, for it exploded where it was supposed to, just above the hill. 800 angry steel pellets showered down, seeking what was legitimately theirs over a 20-metre radius.

There was panic in the ranks and Harry saw the Tiger fighters scramble up the slope. They covered a little more distance and Harry loaded the rocket launcher, on the run, patting Anil on the back to take the shot. Anil stopped, leaned forward to balance and fired. The round dug into the bund and exploded harmlessly a hundred yards ahead. Anil's big chest was heaving at a frightful pace and the way he had dropped distance, Harry worried about getting his toes blown off with the next shot. He ordered Anil to drop the rocket launcher and continue the assault with the AK.

A man was coming towards them, ambling along as if he was out for his morning exercise. As he drew near, Sathish dropped to his knees to bowl him over. He didn't look Tamil, so the men held fire and the Gurkha drew up to Harry. For a man who had been shot at close quarters and had seen some of his friends get killed, he was a study in coolness. Calmly he pointed to the hill behind and narrated the sequence of events to Harry. He mumbled something about being shot and amazingly showed two neat holes on either side of the seat of his baggy trousers—'the advantage of an ill fitting uniform in combat,' thought Harry. The bullet had scraped his arse from end to end, and even that had not rattled the man. Harry wondered if he had any nerves, for having briefed him the soldier now saluted and continued at his leisurely pace. Someone shouted at him to change direction, for he was going towards the jungle rather than to the post and Harry wondered, if he might not run into another bunch of Tigers at the other end. The soldier didn't hear and Harry felt sorry for the Tigers instead, if this small piece of fighting machine was to find himself amongst them, brandishing his unsheathed kukri.

The sheer audacity of the attack forced the Tigers to concede ground and they broke contact. Harry stood looking at the four Gurkha soldiers dead and stripped off their gear and weapons. One didn't have to be Sherlock Holmes to work out the sequence of events. The Tigers arrived at night and patiently waited for the choppers, but ran into the helipad protection party and had no choice but to engage them. They then turned their attention on the small chopper which fortunately was screened by a couple of trees and managed to take off in the opposite direction. The bodies were lying just below the knoll, and the Tigers were stripping the soldiers when the rocket launcher's round disrupted their proceedings. A couple of soldiers promptly took cover in a hut close by and were facing the brunt of the Tigers' fire. Intercepts confirmed two Tigers killed and another wounded. As they say in guerrilla warfare, the man with the cheaper uniform generally wins.

Silvam had hung around in the village till nightfall. He knew anyone making an attempt in the darkness to go across to the post, would in all probability get shot by the sentries and the villagers knew the risks involved. He had arrived at the hillock by a circuitous route avoiding the open ground and the path in front. The night was spent preparing the position and building a barricade of bush and old coconut trees lying around. A mortar position was dug and stamped out and Silvam then gathered the men in the mortar pit and ran them through the sequence of battle, as he imagined it would unfold, in hushed tones. After downing the chopper, the group would split up, while a buddy pair would hold off any resistance and the rest would slip away by different routes and rendezvous at the jungle camp. A man was dispatched to the temple, just below the post, to discourage any attempt by the Indians to send out troops. If he had the numbers, Silvam would have invested the post and annihilated it to a man. He was an experienced campaigner and had forgotten more about aggressive fighting than a lot of soldiers would ever learn in a life time of soldiering.

The group then settled down for the morning to arrive with most of them dozing off. Silvam, however, stayed awake. The village dogs had been disturbed by their movement and were raising an infernal din. He was worried that the Indians might get suspicious and investigate. It was the only flaw in the planning and he cursed himself for not having tied their muzzles. Strangely, it struck him that unlike in India, the dogs in Sri Lanka didn't have a full-throated bark, but would bay most of the time. And a dog howling was considered a bad omen amongst Hindus, for it apparently portends death. 'Perhaps,' thought Silvam, 'the dogs had a premonition about the calamitous future of Sri Lanka or maybe of the post.'

He looked across at the faint lantern light on the Indian post and wondered what the men were up to. It looked quiet enough to give him comfort. He was a day late, for he had received intelligence inputs about fresh troops that had landed earlier to bolster the post strength. He was more worried about the newcomers, for he knew the first bunch to arrive would invariably be the SF guys.

Then his mind drifted to desultory thoughts of home and childhood. He recalled the kids playing football on the ground below which was now the helipad and his killing area. Silvam clasped on to a concrete image of himself as a young boy, sitting on the same hill, watching the game in progress and feeling very lonely. And here he was now, leading some of the very same boys who had mocked him in school.

The hours crawled, like they always did in such circumstances and finally the stars overhead lost their twinkle and faded in the sky that was growing lighter. A sharp crisp smell which comes at daybreak hit the nostrils and a cock crowed in the distant village. The dogs, having exhausted themselves, uttered no cry and none stirred in the village of Kumulamunai. A strong breeze picked up from the sea, rustling through the palm fronds and awakening the weather-beaten windsock, as it flapped dismally, trying to stay anchored to the thin bamboo pole. The post came alive and figures could be seen attending to the morning stand to, a standard operating procedure followed in combat conditions, wherein all troops report to their battle stations in readiness.

The distant whine of a chopper carried across to the waiting men, galvanising them into action. The Cheetah came over the post and then spiralled down to land at a small clearing instead of touching down at the main helipad. Silvam watched in disappointment as it disappeared behind a bund lined with trees. He was hoping for a bigger bird engorged with men, which could be downed before anybody had the chance to get out. He could never forget how they had missed the chance in the Jaffna University operation. In his mind he latched on to images of that fateful night. The sound of the chopper getting louder till it engulfed the sound of their excited chatter, as it landed in the field. The noise of its engines reverberating in the close confine of the buildings. He recalled the smell of dust blowing up from the field and the strained whine of the machine as it laboured to take off under the withering fire it was taking. Some punishment they took and yet they came. He shook his head in disbelief—incredible luck, courage and an extraordinary display of flying had saved the Indians. 'But this time it is different,' he thought. It was broad daylight and he knew exactly where the chopper would land. Briefly he contemplated moving forward and engaging the parked chopper, but covering the open ground under the shadow of the post machine guns was a high risk. He decided to wait and watch.

Then the plan started to go horribly awry, like plans often do when submitted to the ordeal of battle. A section strength of ten soldiers appeared on the track, leisurely patrolling towards the helipad. It was the second flaw in his hastily-prepared plan, for he had completely forgotten about the helipad protection party which always preceded an air effort. Five men walked ahead bunched up and chatting, while the rest walked a hundred yards behind, their rifles slung on their shoulders with the last man herding a couple of stray cattle with a stick in pure boredom. The group in front was in the killing ground just below the hill and Silvam took an instant decision to bag the birds in hand, rather than wait for two in an unknown bush. He gave the order to fire.

The first volley dropped all five in the group and before he could engage the remaining section, the men behind ran into a couple of disused huts nearby. Then a machine gun started chattering intermittently from the post and within a few minutes, the whole post seemed to come alive to the crackle of small arms fire. Most of the fire was inaccurate and went over their heads. He heard the whine of the chopper starting and saw it rise to treetop level. He directed the fire at the bird, and loosened off a few rocket-propelled grenades, expecting it to emerge from behind the tree cover and go sailing over the lagoon, in the direction it had come from, giving him a clear target. But it just disappeared from sight and for a second he thought it had crashed. The next time he sighted the chopper, it was 2,000 feet up and climbing towards the sun.

Suddenly one of the soldiers popped up like a jack-in-the-box from amongst those they assumed were slain and made a run for it. Silvam, with a few fighters, ran down firing at him and the soldier promptly hit the dust. They started to strip the dead bodies off their weapons and usable gear, when suddenly there was a terrific explosion overhead. The element of surprise was over and what was intended to be a simple raid to bag a chopper had broadened into a full-fledged battle.

Anthony, next to him, crumbled to the ground with shrapnel in his leg and Silvam looked up to see one of his men pointing towards the post and urging him to hasten back. He knew other variables were coming into play as the fight progressed, over which he had no control. It was time to slip the cable. Giving a shoulder to the injured fighter, Silvam scrambled up the slope. The firefight was slipping out of his hands. He looked towards the beleaguered post and saw a stream of soldiers running towards them. His first thought was to wonder, what had happened to his man at the temple, for he had been stationed just for this eventuality, to provide harassing fire. The soldiers were gaining ground fast and displaying unusual fieldcraft in the way they moved, going to ground from time to time, so as to provide a difficult target.

Silvam decided to break contact and called to his men to collect the dead and the wounded. He was the last to leave the position and cast a furtive look back at the post, squinting his eyes in the bright sunlight. He could see the Indian troops clearly, for the soldiers had reached halfway to his position and were, it seemed, in consultation with the Gurkha who had made a run and was clearly alive and kicking. Then he wheeled and ran down the opposite slope, carrying the bizarre revelation that the men chasing him were none other than his old acquaintances from the jungle.

An angry and resolute Gurkha contingent immediately poured out of the post with kukris drawn, for a retaliatory response, to the nearest village of Kumulamunai, since the local people had not shared any information prior to the attack on the post. The troops were in the mood for revenge, particularly since the nearby villagers had been living off the largesse of the Indians, in rations and medical supplies. Harry saw the grim faces of the soldiers, as they filed past him on their way to the village and he didn't feel sorry for the locals. If you abet violence, some of it will boomerang back at you. Fence-sitting never helps. And that's how the cycle of violence continues.

In the evening, a solemn assembly gathered for the last rites of the dead soldiers and a hurried subdued prayer ceremony was conducted by the Gurkha pundit in a combat dress. The flickering flames, in the backdrop of the dying sun reflecting on the dark expanse of the Nayaru Lagoon, made for a poignant setting. A thick column of smoke rose up languorously, spreading a pall of gloom on those below. Briefly, Harry's mind drifted to a young woman, a son perhaps or an old mother, somewhere in a remote hamlet, on a distant mountain, in another country, waiting for the man in their lives to come home, and waiting in vain.

Kumulamunai Village

*Death seemed my servant on the road,
till we were near and saw you waiting:
When you smiled, and in sorrowful envy
he outran me and took you apart.
Into his quietness.*
—TE Lawrence, *Seven Pillars of Wisdom*

For the next few days the team was asked to carry out area sanitisation tasks. Then a week later they flew back, to hit the very camp which had cost the Gurkhas dearly in the Alampil jungles. It was a brigade-plus operation and the Indian Army was baying for retribution. The battalion comprising three fighting teams had been split across the island, each operating independently under one of the divisions deployed in Sri Lanka. The entire Bravo Team collected at Kilinochchi and linked up with the Alpha Team which had been flown in earlier from the north of the island where they had been operating. There was great bonhomie as people met each other after months. The battalion had been on the island for nearly two years and there had been few occasions when the teams were thrown together. Generally the only time they operated in tandem was when a camp had to be busted. A joint briefing was held later and Harry was amazed by the content and the candidness of the talk given by the team commanders. Given in any other circumstances, the speech would have shocked the audience enough to boo the speaker off the stage, but here in the context of the time and place, it was absorbed by the listeners with fatalistic resignation.

'Soldiers, you know we have gathered here to carry out one of those ops, which bring more grief on ourselves, than on the enemy,' said Sharma, who was the senior Major. 'But such are the orders and they will be carried out to the letter like always. Each man is a volunteer and has gone through hell to be sitting here. We didn't ask for you, you came to us on your own free will. So no whining for God's sake. You are highly trained, experienced and the best this country's army has to offer. Remember that and don't you let the flag down.'

'We are hitting a camp, so write your letters boys, and finish with your wills—those who haven't,' continued Sharma, as the other officers sat around, nodding their heads in agreement. 'Legs and arms will go for sure, so don't make a racket for God's sake if you are hit. You know it draws fire. You will be picked up, if it's possible, otherwise wait, if you are not in a hurry to meet your maker. Carry plenty of ammo and water, for if the higher ups have their way, we might be settling in forever.' There was some sniggering from the group, the Major ignored it and carried on. 'Those who were in the last big operation of a similar nature where a camp had to be busted in Muttur know the casualties we took. And that was a much smaller camp. This one is the mother of all camps and some of the bigwigs in the hierarchy are present there. You will certainly get a fight for your money. Watch out for mines and IEDs, especially on the trees and one explosion doesn't constitute a minefield,' and he looked at Harry addressing him straight.

'Your troop Harry, sat out the whole fight last time, just because Manohar blew a leg on a Johnny? Make sure they don't sit out this time.'

Before Harry could answer, Zile Singh intruded loudly in defence of the troop.

'It was a minefield sahib,' he retorted, 'we weren't imagining. I for sure was not dreaming up the jerrycan strapped 10 feet away on the tree and nobody knew where the switch was. That alone would have taken the entire troop to kingdom come.'

'All right, simmer down Zile. Nobody is calling you guys yellow,' said the Major, 'just be careful.'

Harry started to get a horrible feeling in the pit of his stomach as he heard them, but drew courage from the men around; they seemed quite calm and resigned. A form of fatalism had set in and the wise man lived for the hour. But Harry was unsure about being stoic and quiet if his legs were to blow off or if his entrails were hanging out. His mind drifted briefly, as he conjured up images of a severely wounded self, propped against a tree, biting his lips in the throes of pain, as life slowly drained out of him. He wrenched himself away from the thought, which threatened to drag him into a quagmire of despondency, and recalled what he had read about experienced soldiers. They had learnt the most important quality of survival in a protracted combat environment—that danger only existed at the exact place and moment of danger, and not before and not after. Imagination is a dangerous virtue, for while it helps some men, it can destroy others when allowed to run riot.

The next day the chopper deposited them in a small clearing very close to where the Gurkhas had been ambushed. There were various small tracks disappearing into the jungle and the engineers had marked the usable path with duct tape and they were warned not to stray for fear of IEDs and mines. On the main path which had been cleared by the engineers, lounged a motley crew of men belonging to the various infantry regiments of the army. Garhwalis, Gurkhas, South Indians from the engineers and joining the party, the SF men.

Heavy firing could be heard from inside the jungle and Harry noticed the tension and fear on every face. A couple of casualties were carried out and he heard an officer screaming into the radio for the casualty evacuation chopper to land. The pilot it seemed was insisting the landing zone was not safe and he wouldn't risk his machine. This was the Indian Army, where the cost of the chopper was more than the life of a soldier, for it was easier to replace the latter. The officer was frantic for he could see his man bleeding to death. He was mumbling something about the boy being the best athlete and wondered how he was going to inform his parents. Harry saw the small chopper hovering in uncertainty overhead and the pilot finally decided to take the plunge, for it came bobbing like a giant dragonfly at treetop level and landed. Harry was not sure if the casualty was loaded, for at that instant the firing picked up and without even a by-your-leave, the bird suddenly took off.

A gunship which had been prowling the sky now came weaving low over the lagoon, like an angry bumblebee and Harry was gripped by fear, just looking at the menacing form coming towards them. The whine of its engines got louder by the second, as it drowned the din created by all the small arms fire and dropped a 2,000-pound bomb, before banking sharply and disappearing from the fight. Someone had the sense to send it home, for the contact was too close for it to support the ground troops anyway. Harry thanked God that he was not at the receiving end, for he had experienced the damage it could wreak. It was all so surreal; the imagery sharp and constantly changing, the sounds loud and the whole scene straight out of a Hollywood Vietnam War movie.

The Tigers, it seemed, were making one hell of a stand against the might of the Indian Army. Rumour was that the Black Tigers were in camp and perhaps Mathaya too may be holed up. The Black Tigers were the LTTE's Special Forces and more. Each person was a volunteer and was handpicked by Prabhakaran himself.

While they waited for orders to move into the jungle, Harry had time to ponder and observe. He watched in an unobtrusive way as a Gurkha soldier whipped out his 12-inch kukri and neatly sliced an onion into four pieces. Then from his pack he took out a packet and carefully pulled out some dry puris. He made a meal of it, chewing slowly, deep in thought. His helmet never came off and he looked haggard and sad, with a faraway look in his eyes. Watching him, Harry wondered, if it hadn't been for employment, would he have joined the Indian Army? It was quite a distance from the hills of Nepal to this back of beyond jungle in Sri Lanka. On a mountain anywhere in the world, this man would have blended with the terrain, a heartening sight, but here in a tropical jungle, he was incongruous. Give him a well-defended enemy position to attack, in a conventional infantry role and this small jolly man, with a protruding bottom and a wobbly gait, would be the most fatal fighting man on earth, but here, he seemed to be out of his depth.

The man caught his eye, smiled and offered Harry his meal. He wiped the kukri on his trouser, ran a finger along the blade and put it back in the scabbard. Then Harry heard a loud greeting from behind and turned to see his old pal Satbir the Jat, grinning from ear to ear and clearly nonplussed about the danger in store. They sat on the narrow path, shoulder to shoulder and exchanged news.

'What bad luck sahib,' he told Harry, 'I was about to go on leave, the convoy got cancelled and then the op was launched. But good, I got a chance to participate or the boys in the company would have given me hell.'

The conversation then strangely veered towards the cost and quality of buffaloes in Punjab and Haryana and Harry's men joined in, turning it into a lively debate. The oddity of the subject amazed Harry, discussing buffaloes at the brink of disparate action, in the middle of a minefield.

A while later, Satbir got up, wearily picked up his rifle, adjusted the helmet and wandered off down the path. The next instant, Harry heard a muffled explosion and saw Satbir lifted off his feet in a cloud of dust next to a decrepit well. He was bawling his guts out and a couple of his colleagues, instead of rushing to help, hung back out of fear of mines. Harry curtailed his natural instinct to jump to a wounded colleague's rescue, checking his stride immediately and reversing back on to the path. 'Stick to the used path,' Harry reminded his boys sitting around, 'for remember, the easy way is always mined.' As Satbir was carried away, Harry saw one of his legs hanging below the knee at a grotesque angle and blood oozing from a head wound. 'Johnny mine sahib,' muttered one of his men from behind, spitting thick yellow tobacco juice, as he shuffled a pack of cards. The Johnny was a locally-manufactured IED, often using a soap box. The plastic signature could not be picked up by the mine detectors and the ordnance carried enough explosives to decapitate the leg below the knee. Once over the initial shock of the explosion, realisation would set in that one had lost a leg and was going to bleed to death, a the man would bawl to high heavens for succour. It was better to have a dead man on your hands, in a combat situation, especially during a live contact, as the wounded soldiers screaming had a tremendous demoralising effect on the others around, often paralysing bodily movement.

This initiated another lively debate amongst them on how Manohar blew his leg in the last op in the Muttur jungles. And what amazed all, was that he was way down in the column, when the Johnny took his leg off and not a scratch to the guys in front and behind him. Harry was sorry for Satbir, a fine specimen of a man and a soldier, but he was more disturbed at the shallowness of his feelings. Clearly, emotions were getting denuded under the constant exposure to violence and death, hardening the man for survival. The only real thought was the satisfaction that it was not you being carted out on a stretcher.

Orders finally came to move in and take over position from the Garhwalis who had been in contact with the Tigers. Harry was burdened with extra ammo and mines and found himself in a head down ass up position. The path became narrower and the jungle thicker. It was spooky and gloomy as no sunlight filtered through the canopy and the fear of mines and IEDs kept one's mind sharp. Harry's eyes were fastened on the track, as they passed a clearing, where a 2,000-pound bomb had flattened all the trees in a perfect radius of 10 metres. A little ahead, he saw smoke from hastily-prepared pyres. The Garhwalis were burning the dead in the middle of the jungle. A hand with a red thread around the wrist hung out limply from under the pile of logs. Clearly the holy thread didn't bring him much luck; perhaps, he didn't propitiate the gods of war satisfactorily. Harry muttered a silent *gayatri mantra* under his breath.

The first person Harry met was a coursemate, Deepak Madhok. Imperturbable by nature, Harry saw Deepak ruffled for the first time. His team had taken casualties and he quickly briefed Harry about the situation. The CO of the Garhwalis was wounded but was still conducting operations with a bandaged arm. They handed over the position to the fresh troops and got out. Harry linked up with the other team which had come in earlier. A dugout, with hastily-piled logs in front, looked safe and Harry settled down in it.

There was no sleep that night as the Tigers and the Gunner officer with the team, kept them entertained. It turned into a duel of sorts. The Tigers opened up with mortars and a heavy machine gun. The huge bullets cracked branches overhead and Harry imagined the impact of collecting one of the slugs. The Gunner Major immediately went on air and called for artillery support. 8 kilometres away, the light guns responded to his request, as they belched in unison their cargo of death. The Major kept giving them corrections in a calm gentle voice, like a father directing his child walking for the first time. The LTTE camp was less than a hundred metres away and the hollow thump of the Tiger bombs leaving the mortar tube carried across no man's land. At one stage the CO had to curb the Major's enthusiasm, as the shells dropped rather close to their own position. A day before, a shell had landed on their own troops, killing a few. It was frightening to hear the high-pitched scream of the incoming shells and then the airburst, as shrapnel tore through the foliage.

Every time the Tigers fired, the Major returned the compliment with interest. Most feared the shelling more than the Tigers by then. But none could deny it was a fine shoot. Through the night, Harry heard both male and female voices from the LTTE camp as they waited for the attack. The women in the camp were all fighters and as good as their male counterparts. The first batch was trained by the Indians and subsequently by Colonel Victor Commander of Mannar, who led them into battle initially. The maximum resistance Harry knew had come from them at Kopay, as the army advanced on Jaffna in the beginning of the conflict. He recalled reading a Sri Lankan writer who had remarked that, 'It was the first time in Indian military history that jawans confronted the opposite sex and suffered badly; an unprecedented phenomenon that shocked the arrogant, male chauvinistic army.'

Harry didn't know if it shocked the rest of the army, but he sure felt sorry for the guys who would perhaps eventually marry them some day.

Nobody was keen to bust the camp, for experience had taught them that the objective would come at a heavy price, as the place would be brimming with mines and booby traps. In one of the camps the unit had raided, other than the casualties, just when the showdown was imminent with the Tigers, on orders from above, a part of the cordon had been lifted and the birds escaped. It was all believed to be prearranged and the Indian external intelligence agency, RAW (Research and Analysis Wing), was blamed squarely for helping some LTTE top brass evade the dragnet. To the last man, the army hated the RAW for its perfidy and double games. Another day and night was spent snarling at each other like dogs, as neither party could summon enough courage to take the fight across. As the firing diminished from time to time, the bold scuttled between dugouts like bandicoots to socialise. Conversation was invariably about the stupidity of entering the camp and suffering unnecessary casualties.

'What's the navy doing!' piped up Hooda, 'patrolling the coastline and pussyfooting, why can't they just shell the bloody area?'

'Too decent by far,' interjected the team commander, 'napalm the place, like the Yanks did in Vietnam. But then we Indians are more worried about what the world will think.'

'And what are we doing here in any case?' interjected the Gunner Major, who was a Sikh officer, 'the further north you go from Madras, the less folks know about this war. Most think we are having a foreign sojourn buying video cassette recorders and gold. What a waste of good lives!'

'Good lives be dammed,' spoke up Sharma from the corner of the bunker, adding a log to the pile in front, 'I have been around on the island for nearly eighteen months and on my last leave home, my young son addressed me as uncle and refused to come to me.'

'Well Sir, can't blame the kid though,' retorted Harry, 'with your long locks and flowing beard, you look more like a drifting mendicant. I wouldn't touch you with a barge pole either.'

'If you have them by their balls, their minds and body will follow,' piped up Hooda, feeling left out of the conversation.

'It's mind and hearts,' Harry corrected him with a chuckle.

On the third day, as first light filtered through the jungle canopy, all the other sub-units were finally in position and the cordon considered sufficiently tight. The dreaded orders were received to escalate the fight and attack the camp. Harry was tasked to stay in reserve and cover one of the exits, for once pressure was exerted, the Tigers' modus operandi had been to split into smaller groups and break out in all directions. The artillery shelling abruptly stopped, there was a lingering pause in the firing and an ominous hush descended in the jungle, the purport of which was lost on neither the defender nor the attacker. It was clearly the signal for the assault to commence.

'The calm before the deathly storm,' thought Harry, as he hauled himself up from his fox hole and exchanged looks with the men preparing for the attack. As he led his troop out, he passed the men getting ready for battle, some adjusting their body armour, checking strapped-up twin magazines for a quick change over, others tightening their bandanas and taking a last sip of water. The regimental doctor was holding fort in situation and had dumped the huge pack he had been lugging behind a couple of thick trees. His medical assistant had done likewise and was busy spreading out the wares of his trade on a groundsheet. Both were climbers and had been old buddies in a couple of expeditions. Harry looked at the piling medical paraphernalia on the ground with a jaundiced eye.

'Hey Doc, hope you don't have to use all that stuff,' he said pausing.

'Not if you guys behave yourselves,' replied Doc Cheema, straightening his back and pulling himself up to his full height of 6 feet, 3 inches. Having witnessed enough bloodshed, his gentle eyes now carried a shadow of perpetual sadness.

'Get your head down Doc, you make a bloody big target and I can see you have carried the hospital on your back. Setting up practice, are you?' retorted Harry, who was clearly fond of the genial giant. Few doctors would have had the courage to be in the thick of the action and Harry admired him for it.

'Well, you know what happened in the last camp we hit,' answered Doc wistfully, 'mark my word Harry boy, there aren't going to be any casualty evacuations happening in a hurry here, once the shit hits the fan. Fight easy and keep your ass safe.'

Harry winked at the doctor and went past. He patted a few backs, shook a few hands, ruffled someone's hair and passed into the gloom beyond, with a prayer on his lips for the men going in and a fervent appeal to his God that if his name was written, then let it be instantaneous. Going a couple of hundred yards further out, Harry spread his men in buddy pairs and they settled down behind the trees, to wait for the balloon to go up.

⊕

Silvam, having arrived in the camp after the raid, had been busy improving its defences. Booby traps and mines were being activated and some of the important stores were hauled out by sea as a precaution. While Mathaya was certain the Indians would retaliate, Silvam believed the last two operations of his had broken their back and it would be some time before they mustered enough courage to venture out of their posts. Barely a week had elapsed since the raid, when Mathaya's predictions came true. The Indian Army was on the move and how! For it was not an army which took a beating kindly and neither was it trained to believe it could remain beaten. A score had to be settled. Reports came in of troop movement from all directions, converging towards the camp. Mathaya knew a fight was now inevitable. The camp was too large to be abandoned without a show of force and while the Indian politician had been warned in the nick of time and diverted back to Jaffna, his own capture or fall would be a fatal blow to the movement.

Mathaya's dilemma to stand and fight as the senior leader was resolved by Prabhakaran, who ordered him to escape at all costs. It was too early in the struggle for his number two to die. The advance units of the army had already made contact with the LTTE's screen defences and were waiting for the reinforcements to arrive. And the reinforcements didn't take long in coming. The moment the engineers had declared a big enough clearing mine safe, the choppers started arriving carrying the Special Forces troops. Taking over from the infantry, the SF teams quickly punched a hole through the LTTE's outer defence cordon and pushed rapidly inwards. Fighting bitterly for every foot of ground against a ferocious band of cornered Tigers who knew the jungle terrain like the back of their hand, the SF teams managed to roll them back, halting barely a hundred yards short of the main camp. There they dug in awaiting further orders. For experience had taught them that any further progress would entail running the gauntlet of booby traps and mines. The first evening Silvam led a valiant counter attack and managed to push back one of the columns, but only temporarily. For the moment Silvam circled back, giving a running fight around the camp periphery, the army promptly moved in again tightening the noose. Once the troops had closed the cordon around the camp as best as they could, considering the difficult jungle terrain, they hunkered down for the night and waited for further orders.

Then the shelling commenced, forcing most of the LTTE men to seek the shelter of the bunkers. They retaliated by engaging the Indians with mortars fired from pre-prepared tree platforms to get overhead canopy clearance. The heavy machine gun, while useless as a weapon for killing in a thickly wooded terrain, had the right psychological impact of stalling the Indian advance. But the constant bombardment was taking a toll and more fighters were getting injured than killed. Sitting in the command bunker, with the shrapnel screaming through the foliage, Mathaya gave his last order to the beleaguered group.

'Anytime now the shelling will stop and the Indians will make their move. Shekhar to stay in camp with a few fighters till the last bullet.' He looked at Shekhar, who acknowledged with pride the order, which was tantamount to a death sentence for him and his men. 'Silvam with his boys and a few Black Tigers from my team, will clear a passage through the eastern side and hold the corridor till such time as the main body with me can get away. Thereafter, at your discretion, make a breakout if possible. The evacuation is to begin now while the shelling is on and while we still have a few hours of darkness, for the Indian dogs will be reluctant to make a move. Go my boys, make them wish they hadn't stepped on our soil and may your sacrifice not be in vain.'

The bulk of the LTTE fighters led by Mathaya slipped out of

camp thereafter, under the cover of the black night. Silvam and his guns covered the escape. Barring the odd shell which landed close enough, forcing them to hit dirt from time to time, not a bullet came their way from the Indians. Mathaya was correct, for most of the Indian troops in close contact were static, under cover, waiting for the shelling to cease. Daylight had broken by the time the last of the fighters crossed Silvam on their way out. Then the shelling stopped and all small arms fire died down. In the stillness of the moment, Silvam looked back towards the camp wondering why Shekhar had also stopped firing and whether the camp was already overrun. With his task over, he decided to join Shekhar in the camp.

Turning around he retraced his way back cautiously, to be confronted suddenly by a bearded Indian face, 30 metres away, silently observing him from across a narrow nala. Silvam recognised the face and also realised that he had a few seconds before the soldier figured out the man wearing Indian Army fatigues was the enemy.

'Madras Battalion Sir,' he said unhesitatingly in Hindi, 'we are in cordon here.'

The soldier didn't acknowledge. His gaze shifted a trifle from Silvam, to movement in the background, where some of the other fighters were gathering. Instantly the face disappeared. Silvam just managed to duck and warn his boys, before they came under fire. He spread his men out and returned fire. He was conscious of two things as he settled down behind an abandoned anthill—that he must keep the enemy pinned down long enough to give adequate time for Mathaya to get away, and second, in a bizarre quirk of fate, he was fighting the same bunch of men, who had often chased him across the island and who were led by an officer whose father had been his instructor in India.

Harry had deployed his troop and taken shelter behind a tree, keeping an eye towards the camp as he expected the Tigers to escape once the assault commenced. Shafts of early morning sunlight penetrated through the gaps and cracks in the canopy overhead, lighting up the jungle floor like some laser beam show. The last vestiges of the night still lingered in the nooks and corners of the jungle. With the guns having fallen silent, it was eerily quiet, with all creatures, big and small of the jungle, having long departed the violence imposed on them by humans. But Harry could sense that the jungle somehow was more alive now, than it had ever been before. Gazing and hostile, the malice of the place was palpable, for it was clearly waiting to unleash violence on the unsuspecting. Harry stood leaning against the tree, inhaling the sharp familiar aroma that permeated a jungle in the early mornings and wondering how his troop would acquit themselves in a fight against the Black Tigers. He didn't have to wait long to get an answer, for he felt their presence, before he saw them.

A man wearing Indian Army fatigues was standing across a shallow culvert that ran in front of their position. For a second, Harry was perplexed, for there were supposed to be no other troops in the area. The man turned and locked eyes with Harry. He looked familiar. 'Madras Battalion Sir,' the man said softly and again the voice sounded familiar. It clicked immediately, for he had heard it last pouring threats to the Jats over a radio, nearly a year ago. It all came back to Harry—the LTTE man they had wounded in the ambush and the one who had got away. Then he noticed movement in the background, confirming his suspicion that they had run into a bloody Tiger patrol. Ducking behind the tree he opened fire.

The fight was vicious, between seasoned professionals, with both sides eschewing automatic fire to trade aimed shots. To the single shots fired by the Tigers, the SF team replied with their signature style of double tap fire; simultaneously firing two rounds in quick succession. Neither party gave ground. Over the sound of gunfire, Harry heard Silvam giving commands loudly to his men. He was an energetic commander and was constantly moving around from one end of the contact to the other. Harry found it unnerving to hear that high-pitched voice in Tamil, running across his front under all the fire. It was psychologically demoralising.

The last buddy pair at the furthest end, suddenly fell back, finding their position untenable under the intensity of the firing. Harry realised what the Tiger commander was doing; he was rolling in the right flank and attempting an encirclement. The man was good and if there had been a bunch of neutral umpires observing the clash, the unanimous decision would have been, one–love, in favour of the LTTE commander. So far he had been dictating the firefight. From the corner of his eye, Harry saw Sathish leave the protection of the tree to toss a grenade. The bullet caught him in the act, smashing his shoulder and the primed grenade fell from his hand. It exploded right when Sathish was trying to retrieve it, the impact hurling him backwards. But the act saved the life of his buddy, who got away with minor splinters to the back.

For a second Harry could not believe that Sathish was a goner. In every op in the previous two years, he had always volunteered to be the point man, as if challenging destiny to do the worst, and now it had. Moving cover to cover, Harry made it across to the supine bloody figure. The fire from across intensified, as the opposition anticipated that efforts would be now made to bring succour to the injured man. His buddy, in spite of being wounded, had already hauled Sathish by his boots behind cover. There was little Harry could do other than hold the dying man's hand, cajoling, pleading and finally in desperation, ordering Sathish to cling to life, for whatever was precious to him.

He recalled Sathish telling him once how he had been conned into joining the SF. As young impressionable recruits in the Madras Regimental Centre, a couple of men had visited them just before they were supposed to pass out. They were tall, lean men, sporting beards and non-regulation hair, tucked under maroon berets, wearing uniforms adorned like Christmas trees. They had an aura of superiority about them, noticeable in their confident gait and informal manner of speech. To a house full of awestruck recruits, they had talked about free fall parachuting, combat diving, climbing mountains and generally doing stuff unheard of in the regular army. Thirty had volunteered immediately, much against the wishes of the Centre Commandant and after a ninety-day probation, only two had been retained. Sathish was one of them.

'And guess what,' Sathish had said in jocularity, 'I ran into Om Prakash sahib in the unit, who was part of the team that had come to the centre. And I discovered he hadn't even done his free fall course while he was confidently wearing the badge on his uniform during the talk. That's what I call being conned.'

'Anything to get the good guys in,' Harry had answered, 'including a bit of deceit, if necessary.'

Harry wondered if things would have been any different had Sathish not made it in the selection. He pulled himself out of the sinking feeling of loss and focused on the situation in hand. Sathish was gone and so would a lot of others, he reminded himself, if he slackened control. 'Most people,' he recalled a saying, 'die at twenty-five, but aren't buried until they are seventy-five.' This man was different, like no other, and had he been offered a menu of the various ways of dying he could choose from, would have still preferred the way he went.

Things were only getting hot and Harry ordered Anil to fire the rocket launcher.

'Where sahib?' Anil looked at him incredulously, 'there is no clearance, it will explode in our face.'

'You see the thick tree with the creeper—that's your target. Hit it. At least it will shut this Tiger commander for some time.'

There was a huge bang as the high explosive round left the barrel, travelling at a speed of nearly 800 feet per second; the warhead quickly armed itself within 15 metres of leaving the firer. Covering the short distance in the blink of an eye, it exploded on the tree. The sound reverberated through the jungle like a rolling barrage. The back-blast of the weapon singed a soldier's leg and nearly unbalanced Anil, who had fired from an awkward kneeling position.

⊕

But the high explosive round had more effect than Harry had hoped for. It exploded above and right next to Silvam, felling him like a cut tree. His face and chest collected the bulk of the steel pellets which riddled them to a state where his mother wouldn't have been able to recognise him. Colonel Silvam was a goner, as life slowly wheezed out of him in laboured breaths. Still shaken from the explosion, a young fighter who was a member of the Black Tiger contingent detailed with Silvam's team, now crawled up to him. Silvam's eyes were still open but the light was slowly going out of them. He looked around at his bedraggled group and gave orders to break contact. As a last act to his fallen comrade, he plucked the cyanide capsule from around Silvam's neck and placed it in his palm. Then picking up Silvam's weapon and radio, the Black Tiger and the rest of the group melted away silently into the jungle with their wounded, to fight another day.

⊕

Harry was amazed at the rocket launcher's efficacy in a firefight. One round had changed the complexion of the fight. A minute ago they were on the back foot and now there was no fight. The Tigers had cleared out in a jiffy. Harry cautiously stepped out of cover and motioned the men to move forward. A few Tiger bodies were lying around and clearly the warhead had done more damage than all the small arms firing. Under the big tree, which had been the target, they found Silvam, badly injured and barely alive. Harry looked down at the battered form of what was once a man, wondering if he was the same guy who he had seen and was he the commander making all the noise? Silvam opened a bloodshot eye and in the brief time he had between life and death, he recognised Harry. He mumbled something and it came out in an incoherent garbled whisper. It drew Harry's attention and he went down closer to the prone figure. Frothy blood poured freely from Silvam's mouth as he struggled with every word. His mind briefly drifted in all clarity latching on to a picture of his young boy running towards him, like always, exuding abounding joy at seeing him after a long time. In the background, he saw his wife, an anxious, worried expression creasing her young face, as if she knew what the future had in store. She was wearing her favourite green sari which he had got for her as a gift from his trip to India. A great sadness engulfed his heart at leaving them alone like this and so early. He knew the wound was grievous and he was a goner. His eyes travelled up and through the gaps in the jungle canopy, he saw a brilliant blue sky lighting up to the birth of a new day. Laxmi would be waking up the boy for school now. His thoughts were interrupted as he felt something sharp on his chest.

Silvam saw the soldier next to Harry put a barrel on his chest and realised, that it was, strangely, none other than his own favourite weapon, the G3 Heckler & Koch, that he had carried and lost in the ambush. All this while he had fretted about killing his old instructor's son, foolishly believing in his immortality while the gods of war mocking his hubris had already charted a different course. Of all the people, it was the old Colonel's son who had finally got him in the end. He didn't feel anything when the bullets finally drilled a hole through his chest for he was already dead.

Harry stood there looking at the corpse for a while, perplexed and wondering at what he had heard the man say in Hindi. Something about paying a debt, and a line, which when translated, corresponded to what a ninth-century Japanese poet had once said, 'I knew I had to go this way, but I did not think it would be so soon.'

Harry was sure he had misunderstood the unintelligible uttering of a dying man, appealing for help rather than quoting a rare verse. An uneducated militant leader couldn't have possibly read poetry. He hauled out a torn plastic camo wallet from the front pocket—the only possession on Silvam—and rifled through the contents. It had a few Indian and Sri Lankan rupees and two faded bloodstained, black and white photographs, riddled by the high explosive rounds. One was a picture of a pretty young woman with her oiled hair parted in the middle and tied in a bun, with a flower tucked in it. On her lap was a small boy looking sternly towards the camera, while the woman wore a forced smile, as if reluctantly following the cameraman's instruction to do so.

In the second picture, a man wearing a thick green jacket and monkey cap, was standing in front of an imposing building, with a mountain in the distant background. A pellet had made a neat hole through the face, making it unrecognisable. But clearly the picture was of the dead man. Harry was about to toss it away, when it struck him as weird that a man who lived in Sri Lanka should be so dressed in winter clothing, and something looked familiar about the building. He cleaned the picture with a bit of saliva and was astounded at the discovery. The building was none other than the Forest Research Institute, in his hometown Dehradun. Harry looked from the picture to the dead man on the ground and found it difficult to fathom the strange twist of this remarkable coincidence. He turned to Zile Singh to share the excitement of his discovery.

'This man was trained by us in Chakrata.'

'Is that so sahib?' answered Zile, showing mock interest. 'I think we should make our way to the camp, the firing has ceased there as well and the injured need to be attended to.'

Harry looked at Silvam's mangled corpse for a while, contemplating his life's journey and the quirk of fate that had led him to that remote jungle at the precise time to meet the man who would be his executioner. Then coming to attention, Harry saluted the brave man.

Gingerly they picked their way across to the camp, carrying Sathish on an improvised stretcher. Every step was a strain on the senses and movement was agonisingly slow. The lead scout walked 20 metres ahead, to reduce the impact of any mine explosion on the others. Their nerves were on edge by the time they heard a command to stop from the perimeter sentry. The soldier stepped out from behind a tree and motioned for them to leave the beaten narrow path, which they had been following. He pointed to the base of a tree next to the track, and ran a finger across his neck. Harry turned to see a crude homemade claymore mine facing them. The soldier, smiling, then pointed up. Hanging from a tree was another improvised device. 'God! How devilish can you get?' thought Harry. The first claymore was just a red herring, meant to be discovered. The killer was waiting above.

The camp was impressively large, with a connected perimeter trench all around and live-in bunkers and command posts made of concrete. The LTTE bodies had been all lined up in a row in the centre of the camp. There were thatched huts, communal for the rank and file and a few single-occupant ones, with a well and a cookhouse in the corner of the complex. Harry heard an excited 'Sir' and turned to see a beaming

Shankaran in olive green fatigues, handcuffed with a rope and under guard. Someone higher up in his wisdom had decided to send him across to contribute his two-penny bit to the clearance op in progress. Shankaran was genuinely pleased to see Harry and kept mimicking the drinking party they had in Kokkuvil. Orders were given not to touch the water from the well, for fear of it being poisoned. The temptation was great as people had been living off a rationed amount of water for days. A large hut with a tarpaulin sheet on top was the store and armoury. The trees and the huts bore shell scars, a witness to the effective artillery shoot. The whole camp was surrounded by a minefield and extensively booby-trapped within.

Fortunately, an alert trooper noticed a suspicious piece of exposed wire, with both ends running underground at the periphery of the camp. He decided to investigate and soon others joined him in unearthing the network. Everybody was asked to evacuate to one corner of the complex, as it became clear that the whole camp may be booby-trapped. The engineers were called in and men trained in advanced explosives from the SF team assisted them. Once the entire lot of wires and explosives were pulled out from all corners of the camp, a shiver ran up every living spine. They were sitting on a powder keg. The entire camp was designed to implode in exactly such a scenario of it ever being overrun. The network of explosives was connected to a pressure switch, hidden below a bamboo pole, erected innocuously at the entrance to one of the bunkers. All that the Tamil Tiger entrusted with the responsibility of setting it off had to do, was to remove the bamboo and expose the switch. Perhaps the man got shot before he could complete his task. Someone unaware would have certainly stepped on it while exploring the bunkers and blown the rest of them to smithereens.

A safe distance from the camp, explosives were placed on trees and an area levelled out for the small chopper to land and evacuate casualties or for the MI-8 to hover and winch up men. The loss had been heavy with serious gunshot and IED casualties. Two men had received a claymore blast to their stomachs and hands and needed immediate evacuation. Doc Cheema had given them first aid and pain killers, but they needed to get to the field hospital at Vavuniya, where the surgeon would patch them up, for the onward journey to the military hospital in Madras. They would then be further sent across to the command hospitals in various corners of the country.

Once the casualties had been airlifted, the fit and the able-bodied stayed another twenty-four hours in the camp, destroying whatever they could. Then the men marched out of the jungle, bedraggled and exhausted, to wait for the birds to pick them up. Harry was tasked to operate in the Kumulamunai belt and boarded the chopper from the very same clearing in which they had landed nearly four days ago. From the open hatch he watched the jungle shrink in size as the chopper rose and then slowly amalgamate into the broadening jigsaw landscape of open fields, villages and the ever-widening lagoon. Harry hoped it was the last time he had to visit the cursed place, which ended the lives of some very fine men before their time.

Gurkha Post—Kumulamunai

When I am rolling, I exist.
When I rest, I am no more.
—Muhammad Iqbal

The Cheetah, a variation of the Aérospatiale SA Lama helicopter, built indigenously by the Hindustan Aeronautics Limited, circled over the post, as it sought to align itself over the landing zone. To the soldiers watching from below, the pilot, it seemed, was unnecessarily agonising over making a perfect landing. And like a hesitant bee hovering over a flimsy flower, he took his time making minor adjustments, to gently settle down on the exact spot marked by a large white H. The door opened to disgorge an odd assortment of people for a military chopper in a combat environment—front-line reporters from various national dailies, carrying their notebooks and cameras. Shradha, being the only woman, was getting all the attention from Brigadier Bhalla who had accompanied the group from Jaffna. The reporters were on an official visit and had spent a few days travelling across the island meeting commanders and civilians alike.

The picture so far had been consistent; peace and tranquility had been stamped on every inch of the land. Then Shradha's journalistic instincts picked up a rumour of a large clash somewhere on the east coast. Over a drink in the evening at the brigade mess at Palaly airfield, she had badgered Brigadier Bhalla to get them closer to the fight. Reluctantly, he agreed to fly them to the post closest to the scene of action. However, he had sternly warned the gathering, raising a finger like a school master addressing some recalcitrant children, 'It would be a brief touchdown, no pictures without my permission and definitely no interviews with soldiers on the post,' he said.

Shradha could sense something big was afoot, for no one showed any interest in their arrival. The post was bereft of any normal martial activity and rather quiet. 'Very unusual behaviour,' she thought, 'for soldiers were always most hospitable and happy to meet civilians.' The few men who went past avoided any eye contact. Her thoughts were broken by the clatter of a heavy chopper which landed below the hillock. A bunch of bearded, long-haired, heavily-armed men alighted. They looked more like Mexican bandits in some Wild West movie, rather than soldiers. Carrying their heavy loads, in single file, they silently mounted the hill to the post.

Suddenly, a tall man broke away from the column and approached her, a big smile disappearing into his thick beard. She looked at him for a second and then threw herself at him, much to the amazement of the others around.

'I knew I would run into you Harry,' she said, holding his hand and beaming. 'Gosh, but you look terrible,' she continued, quite oblivious to the stares they were getting. 'And what is this, are you wounded?' she asked him, with an alarmed glance at his blood-caked battledress.

'Not my blood, but equally precious,' answered Harry, a shadow of grief flitting across his eyes.

'I checked with my army contacts when I landed and they said, you were last heard of in these parts. Did you get my letters?' she asked expectantly.

'Haven't received a letter in a month now. Guess they are chasing me all over the bloody island,' he replied, conscious of the Brigadier's eyes on him. 'Look Shradz, we are passing through, basically loading up on ammo and food. Don't have time and I can't tell you much. But we have been in a big fight,' he whispered. 'Need to even the account with the bastards. Will write you a letter and catch up with you in Delhi soon.'

'Wait,' she said, as he turned to go. Rummaging through her satchel, she pulled out some pictures. 'Got the negatives developed of my last trip. Might be of some use to you.'

With a cursory interest, Harry flipped through the pictures, of jungles, camps and sundry Sri Lankan scenery, which he saw every day and then stopped at a picture of Shradha standing with a short, stout man, in some unknown jungle location.

'Did he limp?' Harry asked, pointing at the man in the picture.

'How do you know?' she answered, looking bewildered. 'His name is Silvam. Seemed a big shot in the hierarchy. Spoke Hindi well and claimed to have travelled in India.'

'Well, his name was Silvam,' replied Harry, 'he met his maker at our hands, somewhere there,' he continued, looking towards the distant jungle. 'He did pick up Hindi in India and this is where the plot gets bizarre. He was trained by none other than my own father, in a back of beyond place called Chakrata. Will tell you the whole tale in more peaceful circumstances over a drink. Take care and don't do anything I wouldn't do kid. Cheers!'

The whine of the chopper's engine was growing and Brigadier Bhalla was impatiently herding everybody towards it. Shradha was the last to hop in and she found herself a seat next to a porthole. The chopper shuddered briefly, like a big wet dog shaking off water and with a final surge of power, it rose up lethargically at first, as if reluctant to leave the ground. Then it circled over the post, gaining height. Shradha pressed her face against the glass, desperately searching for a sight of Harry on the ground. As the chopper made a final turn over the post, she saw a lone figure standing at the edge of the forest. From 800 feet, it was impossible to make out the features of the doll-sized human, but she didn't need to. The man briefly raised a hand in salute and when she looked again, twisting and turning in her seat, Harry had vanished into the jungle. She felt a sense of great emptiness as the emotional bond was severed, plunging her into a profound melancholy.

Having gained a safe distance from terra firma, the chopper dipped its nose and ran forward like a hunted hare. The land below rapidly disappeared, to be replaced by a shimmering sheet of water, as it flew over the lagoon. Engulfed in thoughts of Harry, Shradha sat peering down at the fast-receding shoreline. A small white temple came into view. It was perched on a rock that projected into the sea. A woman and a young boy stood holding hands and looking up at the chopper.

The boy raised a tiny hand and waved, disappearing from sight as the bird banked, setting course north-west for Palaly airfield.

The woman and the child stood in silence for some time, watching the chopper get smaller over the horizon, till it vanished from sight. For three days Laxmi had waited for her husband and now she knew in her heart, he would never be coming back. As tears rolled down her cheeks, she pulled out a small piece of paper from inside her blouse and read the hastily scribbled note in Tamil. A frown creased her young face as she tried to make sense of the message. There was an unfamiliar-sounding name of a man, in a city she had never heard of, in faraway India. 'Dehradun,' she muttered loudly to herself, as she tried to fathom where and how far it would be. At length she looked at the paper in her hand, all the while trying to figure out what to make of it. Then wiping her tears, she rolled it into a ball and tossed it into the swirling water below.

Storm clouds were gathering out on the sea and the wind had picked up. Leading the boy by the hand, she made her way back to the village, from where a keening wail could be heard faintly wafting across in the breeze.

The village of Kumulamunai was lamenting the death of its heroes.

The Wait

Breeze caressed her long tresses,
As fear brought a tremor to her lips.
Her cheeks were flushed with a longing for an uncertain future,
As she waited for him under the palm tree.

Resplendent in womanly glory,
Her eyes glistened with unshed tears of despair.
Dawn to dusk and the sun-rinsed evening changed
moods with each passing hour.
The moon sparkled like diamonds on the endless expanse of water,
And the night came alive to the sound of
a thousand carefree creatures,
Conveying a sense of anticipation for a promise to be fulfilled.

The wind whispered life's secrets,
drawing her heart towards the scorching pit of doubt.
A nightjar shrieked a warning and in the distance
dogs bayed as if to a lost soul.
And somewhere deep in her heart she knew:
'He would never be coming back.'

—An anonymous widow, Sri Lanka

The IPKF Memorial in Sri Lanka

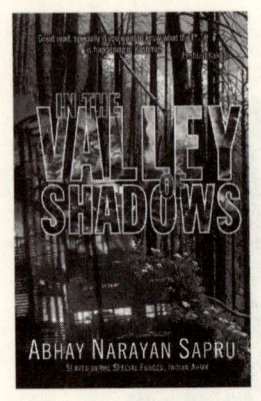

There is a vacuum in the field of war fiction in India and Abhay's book fills it. —*The Hindu*

The book engrosses you and transports you to the beautiful Lolab Valley in Kashmir ripped apart time and again by violence and bloodshed. —*Mumbai Mirror*

The nerve tingling tale of battles between soldiers and terrorists is interspersed with the narrative of love in all its complex shades. —*The Tribune*

The stunning Lolab Valley of Kashmir.

Cold. Crisp. Serene.

Punctuated by the blood curdling violence that rips apart the stillness of this paradise.

Within the militancy torn valley nestles the ravaged lives of the people who inhabit it. And of the men in uniform who fight for their country.

Set against the backdrop of this rugged milieu is the clash of two charismatic leaders—the inimitable Major Hariharan of the Indian Special Forces, and the volatile battle hardened Pakistani mujahid, Sher Khan. Caught in this bitter conflict is the enigmatic Sahira, a local Gujjar girl who has to face her own demons. All of them have journeys that will test their strengths over and over again…

In the Valley of Shadows is a compelling tale of courage and passion and the hatred that an insurgency generates, leaving a trail of destruction and devastation in its wake. Follow the thrilling cat-and-mouse game between two passionate men of war, a chase that only one of them will survive…

In the Valley of Shadows • Abhay Narayan Sapru
ISBN: 978-81-8328-184-3 • ₹295